Alignment With God: The Secrets To Your Heavenly Journey, Spiritual Growth, And Peace.

Book II

<u>The Eternal Tools</u>

By
Mary M.

All Rights Reserved
Copyright © 2007 Mary M.

No part of this book may be duplicated, reprinted, reproduced or transmitted in any form or by any means, electronic or mechanical, including photocopying, recording, or by any information storage and retrieval system without permission in writing from the author.

ISBN 10   0-9822878-0-1
ISBN 13 978-0-9822878-0-4
Library of Congress Copyright Number: TXu001349048

Printed in the United States of America

Second Printing

For Information or to order additional books, email us at
bb@hdnle.com or visit our web site:
www.hdnle.com

Dedication

I would like to dedicate this book to the source of my life. With His loving guidance and His merciful ways, I was able to write an inspired accounting of my faith journey on this Planet.

To all my loving, supportive, and peaceful "Earth Angels", during those weak moments of my life that you have lifted me up, I dedicate this book of Wisdom from God to you. Thank you all, for walking the hard walk with me, side by side with God!

To all other children of God, here's a chance to renew your life and to have faith again…**THIS IS A BOOK THAT IS TRULY DEDICATED TO YOU, FROM YOUR FATHER ABOVE!**

CONTENTS AT A GLANCE

Acknowledgements...v

Introduction.. vii

Chapter 1: Preparing The Spiritual Vessel....................1

Chapter 2: The True Surrender.................................19

Chapter 3: Mankind's Sacrifices..................,................ 26

Chapter 4: The Sharing of True Love......................... 33

Chapter 5: Your True Dwelling...................................40

Chapter 6: The Merits of Living Life for Others............49

Chapter 7: The Exercise of Profound Humility..............55

Chapter 8: The Evolving Spirit...................................63

Chapter 9: The Transformational Phase......................68

Chapter 10: The Miracles Received.............................80

Chapter 11: The Heart Of Gold..................................87

Chapter 12: The Humble Servant................................92

Chapter 13: Carry the Light..97

Chapter 14: The Strength From Within...................... 101

Chapter 15: The Fight From The External Forces........105

Chapter 16: Discernment of the Holy Ghost................111

Chapter 17: Mankind's Dominion Over Earth..............118

Chapter 18: The Quiet and Fulfilled Spirit..................121

Chapte19: The Conclusion......................................125

Acknowledgement

I would like to acknowledge God, for His continued spiritual support during the times of my weaknesses, trials and tribulations. I would also like to thank and honor Him for giving me the privilege to use the wisdom that I have gained from The **Eternal Tools of Alignment** that have worked so wonderfully in my life! And to recognize His unconditional love, guidance, protection, and the loving inspiration, that only He can provide me during those waking, and non-waking hours of writing.

I thank all the Angels and all the Saints of Heaven and of this Planet, for the protection that they have given my loved ones and I. The numerous times that they have been there, to protect those people that matters most in my life. They have helped me tread my walk of life in peace, and in total surrender to God in all the past years, now and for the rest of my life. I am also sending my Eternal Love and my gratitude to all Celestial and Ethereal beings seen and unseen, for the guidance that they have contributed during this beautiful sojourn and celebration of Life!

To this World, thank you for giving me the stage to play my life in **"Alignment with God!"** Thank you also, for giving me the lessons that I needed to learn to grow my spirit, to align myself properly, and to conform only to God's wishes.

I will always treasure the true wisdom that I have gained from such a wonderful experience of learning life. Life itself has taught me to value my many wonderful memories of laughter and tears! It has created for me the beautiful chain of events, which has led me to the pearls of visions before my very eyes.

It has unfolded my future, and the future events that are about to come in the near future of this Planet!

I wish for God's energy to rule this World, and to breathe in it again, another chance to heal. I am also wishing that He would reclaim this Earth again in total surrender to His almighty goodness and encompassing warm Love!

And to all of you, please remember that during those times of our weaknesses, we will together tap into God's greatest strength of His unconditional love and light. For our very own weaknesses are His strength. We will grow our spirits together, to be most worthy of Him and His attention so that in the end, He will always complete us for whatever we need right at this moment, or in the future of our once memorable lives! Remember that our greatest Teacher, who is also our Heavenly Father, is the One Who will lead us to our due course of Life, in another space, another time, another place, another time and space!

To all the lights and love that are here, there and everywhere, thanks again for the profound mystical experiences of living such a wonderful physical and spiritual existence the second time around especially when God is in the midst of it all! I thank you all so much, for the countless Earthly protection, guidance and wisdom, that I have experienced during those times of fear, confusion and for those times of my moments of weaknesses.

Above all, I thank those who will listen and not deny the truth from their lives. Thank You my Heavenly Father, for the wisdom that I have gained from your teachings, and from your Messengers of Lights and Love! I have used your **Eternal Tools of Alignment** in walking my life, and although it was, and it still is a tough walk, it has always managed to help me endure the tests of my time.

Introduction

With the **Eternal Tools of Alignment,** God has shown me the way to the path of enlightenment and wisdom. He has helped me to align my spiritual faith journey properly, and He has replenished the strength of my weakening spirit.

The proper use of the **Eternal Tools of Alignment** has helped me to become a stronger person spiritually, physically and mentally. Living on this planet without the **Eternal Tools of Alignment** will be a tough and a very difficult one, because the depth of total surrender and blind obedience will never be understood. The knowledge and the wisdom that I have learned were good enough to aid me in dealing with the tests of my time. All the wisdom that I have learned, have helped me to adequately shield myself from the unnecessary trivialities of this life's difficult journeys. Now, I can honestly prioritize what is more valuable, and what is most important in my life!

The wisdom that I have learned, from the use of **the Eternal Tools of Alignment** has made me a capable and humble servant to serve God better. The wisdom that I have learned has actually made me a better person to my family, my neighbors, my friends, and most of all... myself. It has made me understand, respect and appreciate Love most as a vital tool of my daily life, and a very important ingredient of my energy giving life on this Planet! With the absence of love in our lifetime, the peace in our spirits will also be very hard to achieve. Love carries with it, the warmth from the lights of God's Heart that will help heal this ailing World!

Love in the future of life, will eventually emote the Universal Healing Energy that will ultimately shield us all from the darkness of our lives! And I thank the Lord for such wisdom.

Without the **Eternal Tools of Alignment,** life itself will be a meaningless direction of unnecessary noise, trivialities, and absurdities. Perception will be deceiving, because the wisdom of proper discernment cannot be fully achieved! **Without the attainment of Godly Spiritual Wisdom thru the use of the Eternal Tools of Alignment, the fall of mankind will be inevitable as a future.**

Faith alone cannot save us from our misdirected walk for so long. Even the winds of time will topple us to the windless journey of failures, confusion and desperations in our lives. With the **Eternal Tools of Alignment** we will begin to die for God, in the hope of rising again; we will be reborn in God's hands and with God's protection. In the future time, we will live with the renewed vigor and zest for Life that can only be imagined, once we relive the future of our lives in good faith and surrendered to the Hands of God! In that bright future, we will live our lives so different from those that are immature in their Spirits. As they continue to ask their endless and meaningless questions and create some noise about our faith, we will have all the answers in our lives to help us endure, the very tests of our time!

We, on the other hand will just have to pray and leave them alone with love, that they may grow their spirits in due time, for the sake of their remaining lives on Earth! As individuals, this will be the time that you and I, will regain what we have lost, and we will together find the treasures in our daily walks of life! This time, in our individual lives, we have actually gained the true wisdom from God Himself!

We have finally followed Him in our daily walks of life, and follow His true commandments in blind obedience to His will! In due time as an obedient Human being, you will become the miracle that God has always wanted to happen on this Planet. You have successfully handed over your freewill and your control to God. You have finally renewed your life! Now, you have totally accepted Him as your personal Savior and Father. And this time, in your present life, you have trusted Him with your life and with everything on this Earth!

The Eternal Tools of Alignment has paved a clear passageway to the Lights and the Love of God that will direct you straight to your place in His Heavenly Kingdom! When we become the obedient Children of God, we will thrive in the positive light of our Strong Spirits because right then, we will be equipped with the tools of God. As our lives changed, our spirits will mature for good! We will endure the tests of time that will be presented before us in the future with no qualms. In the future time of mankind, we will succeed where others will fail, because God will always be on our side! He has given us the most sought secrets to prepare ourselves and to properly align with His ways in this book, so we can all journey together in the light and in the warmth of His love!

With His guidance, we will never be lost again. Our faith journey in this lifetime will be an amazingly wonderful, memorable and most enchanting one with a bittersweet ending of peaceful memories of a strong Spirit who is one with God! We will always be centered in our lives, and we will be at peace with ourselves! Our faith will not waiver anymore, and our hearts will not be faint. Our spirits will be very strong, because it is anchored firmly into the ground held by God's unconditional love and powerful wisdom!

God will replenish what we lack at any moment of need in our time, and He will always provide the protection to keep us from any harm. Peace will reign again in our hearts at last! Come join God and start your journey using His simple tools of Alignment.

Do not complicate yourself with unnecessary trivialities in life. Prioritize your life because this is the right time to do it! At this time, put your priorities in order and focus to keep your peace from within you at first. Give the commitment to start slow, and humble yourself as an empty vessel for God to shower His blessings in your life! And let Him fill you up with the bliss of eternal life, happiness, and powerful spiritual wisdom to grow you Spirits. Digest the wisdom and the knowledge that you have acquired as if you were thirsty and hungry for more. Start slow but do not run with the knowledge. Walk your baby steps in profound humility. Humble yourself. Believe in your faith and walk slowly one step at a time and live your lives one day at a time.

The Eternal Tools of Alignment although given to you as a privilege, will require that you first believe in the existence of the Holy Trinity! God the Father, The Son and the Holy Spirit as One! Without faith you will have a meaningless journey! Begin your journey right, and you will always end up right with any direction that you will undertake in the future of your life! With God, you will never be lost again.

In God's kingdom, there is an existence of a Throne and the Celestial and Ethereal Beings. Without believing that this place and beings really exist, it will be hard for you to receive their communication and also receive their messages. Most spiritual encounters are mystical and are beyond any of your Human capabilities and probably comprehension.

The only way perhaps for you to understand it… is to use your **discernment** from **The Eternal Tools of Alignment.** Without establishing your faith first and believe that God truly exists; it will be very hard for you to start even learning the barest minimum of God's wisdom! When you close your mind from learning the wisdom of God from the very beginning, it would be very hard for you to even discern through your Spirit the **Ways of God**. You will start with a state of disbelief with whatever you will be trying to accomplish. Ultimately your narrow minded thinking will only help to destroy your already stagnated and ailing Spirit.

God does not want to be placed and cornered in a box. When you practice your faith without gaining the right wisdom, you are only fooling yourself. In the due time, you will accomplish nothing and you will also gain nothing but a waste of your time! If you do not even have faith to begin with, do not even waste your time learning the **Eternal Tools of Alignment!** The time is not right for you. It will not be right for you to force yourself to learn something that you cannot even begin to accept from the very beginning. Learning the **Eternal Tools of Alignment** will demand a full commitment from you. Without committing to start right, there will be no sense to even begin the journey of learning the right way. The same saying will be true for you, if you are not ready to fight evil yet, do not do it! In this case, w hat you do not know can hurt you. Do not attempt to challenge what you do not know. The Universe is full of presence that is more powerful than you, and what you know! Without God and His wisdom, it will be harder to choose and fight the right battles. And if you fight the wrong ones, it could be a very dangerous thing for you. It will surely be a definite death of your spirit if you do so, and the untimely demise of your soul!

To understand and learn the lessons from the **Eternal Tools of Alignment,** one must be committed to practice it the right way, or you will end up more confused than when you first begun. One very important commitment is to start believing that God do exist because you will need His protection at all times.

God is a total embodiment of Pure and unconditional Love. In Him, you can trust. That with Him, you will not imperil your life, because he loves you more than you can even dare to compare with any kind of love that is humanly possible on this World! To understand Him is to believe in Him at first!

To receive Him in your life and to teach His ways is for you to prepare a sanctified body and a clean environment, because He is Holy and very Sacred. It is not fair to call on God and expect Him to wallow with you in your filth! When there is cleanliness, there is Godliness! God is never present in a filthy environment. Be aware that this time there is no getting around your excuses anymore. So clean up the house where you invite God to sit down with you! This time, it is imperative that you do not fail Him with what He expects from you. Do not worry about being imperfect because He knows that too. Just do the best that you can and righteously and humbly! Then, leave the rest in His hands!

When you are ready, He will seek you out. You can seek Him any four corners of this World, but if you are not ready for Him, you will never find Him! This is the truth that you must remember and put this seriously in your heart!

The Eternal Tools of Alignment will help you grow to be ready and be worthy of God! The tools are His ways of telling you that He truly loves you and He is giving you a chance to renew your life. Accept God and surrender your will to Him and to be ready for Him at all times. He is helping you to see the light that only He can provide for you!

As you practice **His Eternal Tools of Alignment** and truly align yourself in your actions, and in your deeds, remind yourself to be humble at all times. Be vigilant of His presence in all aspects of your life! Welcome all the wisdom that you can take to help you in your struggles with life!

When you are ready, He will manifest in your life. There will be beautiful changes and miracles that will happen to you, your family, your neighbors, and your friends. Positive things will start to unfold before your very eyes, and progress in the direction of your life will be inevitable.

You will smile as you have never smiled before! What a wonderful blessing for you in the end! Start to prepare now and be serious about your commitment with God. If this is the first time that you have been serious about doing something, this is it! Be serious, because this time is the right time to recover what you have lost in your life that really matters most to you. God will hold your hand to recover those lost times!

Do sacrificial fasting, be praying more, and be a nicer person to your family, friends and to your neighbors. Clean up your acts towards your neighbors, family and friends. Rid your body and your mind of all the evil and negative stains that you have accumulated for such a long time! And pray for all your inequities and disobedience in the past, present and the future of your life!

There will be all kinds of communications; Mystical and Spiritual messages that will happen, especially during the time of fasting.

The weaker you are physically, the stronger you are in your spirit. Be wary of the kinds of messages that you may receive and be prepared to discern it with the help of your mature spirit!

As you continue to fast and pray, be aware of the co-existence of good and evil. Be wary of the darkness that will try to stop and intimidate you! Discern properly, with the use of the **Eternal Discernment of the Holy Ghost!** Call God and His Angels for protection and help. The confusion will start when you do not learn to start right and have anchored your spirit firmly with God in profound humility!

Without proper discernment and the right faith, the messages that may be given to you will sometimes be something that could deceive and confuse you! With the use of the **Eternal Tools of Alignment**, you can learn it the right way; and you will begin to receive the wisdom from God!

When you use the **Eternal Tools of Alignment**, if at any time that it becomes an overwhelming task for you at that particular moment, slow down, step back, and try to regroup yourself and ask for God's direction and wisdom. God and His Angels will be present at all times, watching over you as you pray for His guidance and protection during those difficult hours of fasting, prayers, and learning.

Always use **Love** and **Profound Humility**, as a ready tool to deal with the everyday dealings of this Earth. And start to get God's good graces in your life!

Love will work hand in hand with **Humility**, to give the light to your confused and growing soul! Do not worry if others will mock your changed ways, what they do not know, you do! They have only to focus on their own inequities to be able to understand the depth of your commitment and personal relationship with God.

Know that with God, you are well blessed and protected in your daily walks of life! Believe that you are complete and self-contained when you are with God. Let Him always anchor you and stabilize every decision that you may have to make.

Accept the things that you cannot change, because with God, with a single wave of His hand all your worries will disappear into thin air! As you love and respect Him, He will honor, treasure, protect and love you always! Be an obedient child first. Do not hurry the wisdom that must be slowly learned and earned first. You will gain a substantial amount later on.

Take your time and treasure every step that you may take. God will guide you in your walk to Spiritual Maturity! Use these tools! You might be surprised in what it can do to your life, your peace, your family life, and your love life as a whole.

Be thankful for the chance to learn His ways! He is calling you, so answer Him back…He is there waiting for all of Eternity!

Chapter 1

Preparing The Spiritual Vessel

Come Holy Spirit!

Come Holy Spirit!
Open my wings and spread the good news of Mercy!
Bestow upon me the Humility of my Soul,
Share with me the Happiness of Love!
Enlighten my confused Life,
To Surrender to you the Truth!
Oh Holy Spirit!
I bent my knees and pray before you...
And I surrender my Life!

For the first time ever, prepare yourselves to the most significant journey of your lives! Welcome the grace that is only coming from the Savior Himself, your Eternal Father in Heaven!

Welcome all to God's secret wish for you - **His Eternal Tools of Alignment.** These are indeed the tools of pure and unconditional Love! These are the tools that will help your stagnated Spirit to mature to reach your ultimate Spiritual growth and help you in your quest for life!

Empty your half-filled containers and vessels and leave some or most room for God to work in your lives. Let him fill it all up with the gifts that you are privileged to receive. You will now embark on a journey of a walk with God. Do not walk half full with Him and remember to receive the fullness of His grace! Do not limit your vessel to only accommodate a little of the entire world of wisdom that He alone can bless you. You must be in total emptiness to even start the right walk.

Hold on to His loving and warm Hands to direct you back to the center of your once lost life. Alone in your walk with him; you must remember that profound humility and the nothingness of your own entire existence will help you start anew and in the right direction of your beginning journey. As if to die and to be reborn again, but this time, with God in your life! At this point in your journey, you do not exist anymore for yourself because you are not the focus of your so-called real existence anymore.

This time in your life, the "I" factor in yourself will be taken out and God is the first and prime focus, and your personal relationship with Him will be your first priority. You will now embark on a new journey with God as your loving guide. You will now be directed towards a new awareness that you are to become His well deserving warrior. This time, you will exhibit a good behavior towards His other children, and be noticed only as His good and obedient child.

This is the time that you will surrender your free will to be utilized by God alone. You will be born again in the truest meaning of being reborn, reborn for servitude and the determination of a strong soldier serving only his true Master. In blind obedience you go, for deep in your Heart, you know that this time, your true Heavenly Father will walk with you. Armed with love and a stronger Spirit, you will continue to grow and continue to thrive on this Planet with a new hope and an added determination for a good future in a very well deserved manner!

Armed with the highest form of ammunition of Love and God's Lights, you will proceed to walk with the determination to battle a war that this time is not your choice, but God's. Let God handle what you cannot handle. Let Him change what you cannot change, let him help you to accept the fact that not all the battles have to be won but only the right ones, and let God carry you in His protective and Loving Arms all the way through.

Ask God's presence in your life and pray for Him to lead you the way! Make Him choose the right battles for you. Above all, humble yourself before Him at all times. Adore Him with all of your Heart! After all, He is your great Teacher and Protector at all times! Let Him guide you only to His ways that will ultimately lead you to His Kingdom in Heaven. Start your journey with a sanctified body. Invite God inside your clean house to sit down with you. In profound humility, honor His presence in utmost reverence and in profound humility always!

You are now in the fold of the King of all Kings! Prepare the vessel to be worthy of His attention. The stain that you have acquired from years of negativism, misdirection, and misgivings in your life will slow down and deter the speed of God's blessings to start pouring in your now blessed life. Empty the material vessel as well as your spiritual vessel for God to start His work today, in your life! Be ready to receive as much as you can. Handle the gifts as it comes without fighting it and let it flow freely. Once God touches you, His wisdom will be poured into your life and you will not be in a position to oppose it. What is done cannot be undone! Just be happy to receive all of His blessings that will be poured unto you, your friends and your loved ones!

Leave all the misgivings behind; those were the things of the past. Start a fresh journey with God. With joy in your heart, welcome the light that will open more positive doors that you have never seen before and then love your way till the end of your time! Embrace the new directions and the positive changes that will significantly affect your present and future life.

You will ultimately experience some good changes, in the way you will deal with other people in your life. You will now walk a different walk than what you're used to before. And as you go, learn God's wisdom by heart! Take time to learn slowly, all the wisdom that will be given to you in the future will be something that you deserve and can handle easily. It is not forced into you. With God, nothing is forced! But you will have to work harder to get His attention and earn His wisdom.

All of God's creations were given the gifts of freewill and they were never forced to worship God. When God gave the "**Gift of Freewill**", He promised that this is the gift that He will never intervene. He wanted us to use it freely for whatever purpose in life, but His only hope is that, we use it for a good purpose to help us grow our spirits to maturity!

Armed with the knowledge of the **Eternal Tools of Alignment,** extend your hand to God now. Let Him be welcomed with all your heart in this walk. Make sure that you are deeply committed to the positive change that is about to happen and that He is truly a part of this growth in you.

God will work first by taking you out from your own noisy existence. He will give you peace to rule your heart and mind. Then, He will proceed to shower the true unconditional love that has been missing your entire life. As He does His part, do your part with regards to your Spiritual and Physical cleansing. Be deserving of such hard work and attention from Him. Be aware of the fact that God is doing all these for you because He loves you, and He wants you to experience an easier time on this World. Abide by His rules.

God's rules are nothing to destroy you but instead, to strengthen you in your own personal quest for life. Remember also that there is no permanence in this lifetime existence. This is a temporal life! Nothing of this Earthly existence is permanent and constant! In due time all will come down, and we are going to be witnesses before Him to answer the final judgment of how we have lived our very own lives!

At the end of our time, we can only hope for God's forgiveness for all the sins that we have committed against Him. We can also hope that in the future, He will give us the pardon and the complete absolution for all of our sins and disobedience to His commandments. Let's face it. This is the reality of our true existence! In the future, we will be begging for mercy for what hurtful things that we have done to the rest of our brethren. So if we want to change, why not start now and simplify our very complicated and misdirected lives. Start the positive changes in your daily walks of life and stop living in a lie.

Stop pointing your fingers at everybody else around you. Take charge of your life and take responsibility for all of your actions may it be a small or big! Above all, start taking responsibility for everything that you do.

Every bit of freedom that we enjoy must not be smeared by carelessness, utter arrogance, and inconsideration to other people's feelings. Be mindful of other people of God around you. They are equally special to God like you. Reclaim your true identity as children of God. Even if you have been weakened by the tests of time, deep down inside your heart, you have always known that sometimes you were also at fault. You have suffered in the past because you did not know any better. But this time you knew that at last, you have been saved. Just be humble, in profound humility God will lift you up to the Heavens above!

Accept your faults. When you call Him fervently, God will be active again in your life after you pushed Him away from you for so long. Let His guidance and wisdom now flow through you freely and allow and trust Him to guide you properly. Let His wisdom guide your every decision.

Trust that only He can guide you and lead you to the right battles to be won that will only strengthen your Spirit, instead of destroying it! This time you know that you are not alone in your walk. Although walking with God can be as painful as it can get, just be ready to trust His ways to shield you from the pains of your life. The truth of His wisdom will sometimes hurt, and the road to the road of justice is not as wide and pleasurable of a journey, but it is all a part of the life of a growing soul to become the most worthy of a Spirit for God!

Accept the fact that right now you are in your baby steps, and you are aware that the learning in itself is as hard as the walk! You are living in a World full of distraction and noise. Even to just feel and hear your own heartbeat and trying to figure out what your heart dictates is such an effort in the present times of commotion and chaos.

Do not allow any more delay in growing your spirit properly, because in the future there will be no more excuses that will be accepted by God! Be prepared for all times; be very vigilant, for a lot of sacrifices will be asked of you in the future. Live each day, as if it were your last!

With the proper use of the Eternal Tools of Alignment, you will be exposed inevitably to a new reality that although will broaden your wisdom, will also test the strength of your spirit. Be prepared and be ready at all times. In preparing yourself to learn the ways of God, also prepare yourself for the tremendous amount of challenges that will occur in your life that will hinder you from growing your spirit properly. The other dark side of an allowed existence will not be caught sitting down, while you work for God. If you open a little door for him, he will take every opportunity to deter and stop you in your work for God.

Remember that an evil deed is not from God; so do not blame God for your evil misgivings and neglectful ways. You will ultimately become God's true son or daughter in the end, but not without the price! There will be some degree of expectations as well to come from you. So, do your part wholeheartedly and without expectations. As you have been lost a long time, God expects your commitment and responsible action as a sign of your positive change to redirect your life back to His blissful ways.

Your good deeds for His other children will definitely make Him notice you! And He will ultimately give you the merits for such good deeds. For such a long time in your life that you have disobeyed, now you will be working harder to prove that you are ready to accept God and make the necessary sacrifice that is expected of you. You have violated His trust and confidence in you before, so now is the time to earn it.

And because you have been spoiled by this physical and material World, you might have lost track of taking responsibility for all your actions, small or big it may be, do not be afraid this time to take full responsibility. God only expects total honesty, full responsibility, and total commitment from you.

The journey will not be hard if you at least try to change and learn slowly. The guidance of Alignment **With God** will help to redirect you back to the center of your once lost life! During the first stage of your journey, remember to use the **Eternal Tools of Alignment** first. The Eternal Tools will aid you in aligning your life back to God's fold. God's wish for you to change is definitely in this **Eternal Tools of Alignment** book. Align yourself with God, by being the good example of giving love to other people in your deeds, in your thoughts, and in your words and follow the tools that God has given you in this book in blind obedience.

Obey, surrender and empty your vessels to be used by God. An empty spiritual vessel does not just mean carrying few baggages, which will hinder and slow down your beginning journey. If you carry a lot of negative baggage on your shoulder, let them go before you take an almost perfect walk with your Heavenly Father. Throw away the garbage of your life that will slow down the speed of your spiritual growth.

Do not be deterred by the wrong priorities in your life and start your journey properly by putting the right things in proper order. Put God in the midst of it all. Then go with God's ultimate blessings of grace and wisdom to help you.

Alignment with God is a pure journey indeed, and only God knows when to reveal Himself to you when you are ready. Remember that as you go, He will not proceed in your time, but His own perfect time! Instead of searching for God, go up to His level of expectations about you, and let Him come openly and meet you halfway. This is the way that God works in our lives. Then always prepare a clean venue for God when He enters in your life!

This is when cleansing of your material and spiritual vessels will begin. Fast for your spirit and get rid of so many wants and needs materially. You cannot just come to Him that easy, and Him doing all the work for you. Not anymore! This time you must prove that you are worth His full attention, with all the ways that you have shown positive changes, and in the way that you walk your daily life with love and hope!

As you make progress in your learning, God will show you the way to His loving Heart. He will give you the enlightenment and the ways to discern the right path of your life and ultimately bless you with His Wisdom.

In profound humility, you have to prove to God that you have humbly accepted your place at His side, and you have accepted the wisdom of the true meaning and purpose of your life. Let Him guide you and be ready. His time is different from yours and He will come to you, as usual, in His own perfect time!

Expect less of Him and more of you. You have disappointed Him for such a long time that you have to prove harder now as to how deserving you are of His Love and wisdom. Expect this second chance of your life to be a determination to change for the better and an ultimate chance to experience God in your life again!

Believe that things will change but sometimes not according to what you would have like to experience, but how He wants you to learn from the experiences. Let God's Wisdom flow freely in your life and listen.

Let it give you the direction to find Him! Exercise patience. It is one virtue God wanted you t have always and hope that He will prevail in your life.

When you distance your life from evil, it will be a life changing change for you, because you will be throwing darkness back to oblivion where it really belongs! You will refuse to feel hatred as you do before, but instead, you will use Love as your only ammunition for all your battles ahead, and to win more souls and guide them back to God's side.

God will complete all your needs, so you will have the feeling of abundance in your life and your Spirit will be at peace and well fed. You will soon forgive your enemies and you will forget the pains you once had, for now, it is only God's pain that you will consciously carry. Good deeds will be part of your life, because your mind and heart will be in total agreement to do nothing but the righteous things. What you have doubted before will now be clear.

The peace that you have never experienced before will be part of your solemn walk. A new path will slowly and clearly manifest before your eyes and a better direction of life will be obvious to your sight. A direction that is full of the Lights and Love from God and hope that your Spirit will rise again.

Hope will continue to inspire you to do the best for the other children of God. This time you look at the other children of God in a different and compassionate light. Your sensitivity and consideration for other people around you will be heightened as if such an experience will be new to you.

Preparing the spiritual vessel is like finding the rarest of gems in the middle of an ocean bedded in the bottom of the sea by millions of big rocks. How that gem will be selected is truly dependent on the quality that has been produced after the battles of time. It will definitely glow in due time and will be noticed! After all, it had become the rarest gem in the rough! Personally for you, deep down inside you always knew, that you are that special gem who is just waiting to be unearthed!

After all you are made in the image and likeness of God. This is also the reason why every one will be given their equal chances. Your chance is right now with this book of secrets from God! So rejoice for you are one of the lucky ones who hold the secret ways of God that is intended just for you. How this gem will respond and endure through the battles of change and of time will truly depend on the outcome in its due course.

Rest assured that you are still the rarest of the gems in the World, for in God's loving eye, you are still His most beloved and most special and adored child! There will be tests of the spirit of course, and the future will depend on each individual rarity and gifts of survival.

Now that you have the **Eternal Tools of Alignment,** take advantage to learn from Him directly! You can even learn it in your own time and pace. God will be waiting for you patiently. Many are called indeed, but only a few are chosen in the end. If you are given an opportunity now to learn God's ways and you won't take it, you will e sorry for the rest of your life. If one can survive these tests in flying colors, God will surely honor him or her with His very presence and love. And the lucky ones will be endowed with God's wisdom. Preparing the Spirit for growth, and the Physical vessel is a major task at hand because we are living in this material World. This Planet is ailing, because it is occupied with the most number of materialistic inhabitants.

Now, we are what we have become. And we have viciously failed our very own Spiritual growth. We have become so needy because we also have become very greedy. The need and the greed that we have experienced in this lifetime are endless. We can't just be content and can't just be satisfied. The more that we want, the more that we need! This is the story of our present lives in this materialistic existence!

We do not live a simple existence anymore. We have complicated our lives to utmost confusion and inconsideration. We have become cold even to our own neighbors. We want it all and nothing can deter us from our selfish quest for the nothingness of this life! After all of that, we still end up with nothing to gain, as we are in the risk of losing everything of essence! So our lives are just wasted in the emptiness of time and the nothingness of our immature Spirits!

This highly physical and materialistic World that we are living in is the reason for our failures in life. We have not prioritized properly the needs and the wants in the order of the most importance in our lives! We are lacking the foundation of starting right because we have refused to put faith back in our lives.

Fortunately, the time has come for you and I to be given another shot at a good life with God, because He is now boldly calling all His obedient children to gather around and return back to His fold and to invite all of us to practice our lives in the ways that only He can provide thru this book of **The Eternal Tools.**

God has made it simple here for you to understand that although He agonized your need for power and self-recognition, your need to preserve your pride, and your ultimate need to satisfy your ego, God does love you for all of Eternity! And He will still wait for your return patiently and unconditionally.

In this book, He is giving you that particular chance, to turn around and really simplify your complicated life, and only sort out those needs and wants that will matter most to your growing Spirit in this lifetime!

God wished that you could use your innate tool that He has given you, which is the light within yourself. The light of your Spirit that He alone gifted you and that you can ultimately tap into to be able to make a balance decision when you need to

. You must prepare the very important Physical Vessel. Our physical body encapsulates our soul. It is this body that we have focused so much importance. A little imperfection in any part of our physical appearance will drive us to take the initiative to do whatever we have to do to preserve it. But this is our lower self! It is this lower self-existence about us that we have focused so hard. We have to make sure we look good in our skin-deep perception of beauty. Looking good physically makes us feel so good.

We are so naturally physically and materially oriented that we have forgotten our hungry spirits or our other higher selves within us. These shallow skin-deep moralities of life that we've lived in have distorted the way we value and look at ourselves.

We are misguided in the way we think of our essence as Human Beings. We have actually continued to live in ignorance because we have not recognized our faulted focus. On and on we go with our misdirected lives. The shallower our actions are, the more confused and dissatisfied we are and the hungrier our spirits have become! We are continually marching down the pit of oblivion and total distraction!

On top of it all, the most important part of our higher self, which is our Spirits, are now also being compromised. We have to satisfy our physical needs and senses. We have to make sure that we continue to strive perfection in this part of our lives; our so-called beauty does not lie in the eyes of the beholder anymore, but fall into the arms of bewilderment and nothingness.

On the other hand, if we are true to ourselves, and we truly walk with God in the above manner as we have claimed, we sure are living in a World full of hypocrisy! We are living a way of life that is not really what we profess to be living in. A life of Hypocrisy now becomes your life in reality.

We are living in a lie, and we have refused to take responsibility for the wrong actions that we have taken. Like a slap to God's face and a big blow to our faith, we have continually violated God's trust because of so many excuses that we have to make to cover the tracks of our lies!

Our Heavenly Father although an embodiment of love, understanding and forgiveness, does not work with our limited thinking and our blatant disregard for His rules. Although God is all forgiving and all merciful, He also expects us to be mature enough to take responsibility.

Even God's teachings of blind obedience do not always mean not discerning the right source properly. God always understands our imperfections, but He also expects us to rise up from above it and grow our spirits the right way. He will never condone our deliberate arrogance and our blatant disregard for His rules. After all, we are endowed with His gift of freewill.

We all have to take the responsibilities and consequences of our actions. The time is now. The chance is given and we have to take it for our very Spiritual sakes! Amidst the noise that we are in for so long, this is the time to attain our well-deserved peace.

A lasting peace at last, but we still have a lot of work to do to earn back God's trust! Let's redirect our faulted focus, and strive harder to be more obedient Human Beings for the first time. It is not too late! God is still waiting with so much unconditional love and let us not forget it!

To prepare the stained Physical body, one must clean it through understanding the source of staining. Where you are going to start cleaning is all up to you, but you must make a commitment that is true to your self and to others involved. Above all, you must be true to your commitment with God. The body can be stained by the kinds of food we eat, the kinds of drinks we drink, the quality and the amount of food and other things we put inside our body greatly affect the staining of our physical body. Physical staining can also clog up the Spiritual opening.

This is why we have to spiritually and physically clean our body by sacrificial fasting and praying. The Spiritual staining is due to our evil ways, whether it is in our thoughts or in our actions. We have followed the dark side and his dark ways for a long time that our Spirits are almost dying at the present time and looking very black. There is a spiritual opening in each and every one of us. This opening can be clogged by food and fat and filthy other things we swallow. The closure of this opening because of the above reasons will hinder the grace that should have normally flowed inside our physical vessel in order for us to receive the proper spiritual experiences.

The proper reception of a spiritual experience or encounter depends on how well we have received it. In our spiritual staining, the spirit has also been stained by the association and contact of the negative influences and stimuli around us.

The hurt and the harm that you have done consciously or unconsciously to others will always mark your spirit black and until you go back and straighten it, your sins will seek you out no matter where you hide! So there is no point in running anymore. Running with life without taking responsibility, and pointing fingers to others when you can humbly apologize, are some of the reasons for concern regarding spiritual staining in progress.

You have to be a man or woman to stand behind all your actions, so you will not harm and stain your spirits directly. God has made us in His image and likeness and we also have the capability to experience and expand our wisdom and sanctity only through the Spirit. A sanctified body and spirit can discern any spiritual encounter properly.

Without true sanctity and the proper understanding of its place in our mission, will definitely be risky, and will mislead us to the wrong directions from our true journeys in life!

We must be determined to walk straight back to God's loving mercy to help us receive the true grace in our lives that only He can provide for us. Anyone can receive any spiritual encounter, but it will not be discerned properly if the body and the spirit are not properly prepared for such an experience! Also, our refusal to relinquish control and to cede surrender of ourselves entirely over to God's protection and love will close a door that could have open a beautiful chance to a spiritual and mystical encounter with God.

If you do not have faith, do not even attempt to begin your spiritual journey. Surrender at this point is a must. So that this time, you receive and believe God beyond any humanly possible reasonable doubt that He truly does exists and He is part of your life! Embrace His truth with all your heart and offer everything and anything about you!

Surrender your all to your Heavenly Father and that is also including the total surrender of your freewill! If you are surrendered to God, it will be a stronger spiritual experience with little or no resistance. How you may ask, why prepare a sanctified body? Well, if God is Sacred, so can You! After all, He made you in his image and likeness. You have to also remember that The God in Heavens that I am talking about is a Holy God! Therefore, meet his Holy Spirit with your pure One!

You have to be deserving of his love and guidance and you are responsible to clean your acts before Him. There are a few ways to clean a stained Physical and Spiritual opening. You may, or you may not practice it according to any order, but these steps are essential in the proper preparation of a human body and its higher spiritual self to receive God and His Messengers in your life. Cleansing is an essential part of the tools of Alignment. Without the right preparation of your lower, (Physical) and your higher (Spiritual) self, there will not be a clear direction to your beginning Spiritual walk with God! You may wonder why there are so many rituals and why is it that God is not making it so simple for us to follow. The answer to your question is really simple: this preparation for alignment is really just the basic step to help put you spiritually back to the center of your life!

Your past life have been lost to oblivion, because you have not followed God's rules in the first place anyway. And in the end, you have not gained the wisdom to direct your life properly. The Eternal Tools that is given to you now is a way for you to get a chance to have another shot at life, but this time, with God's help.

God is now unveiling the simple secrets to be living your life the right way, and to help you gain the wisdom and help you in your sojourn with life! It is God's fervent hope that at least this time, you will listen to Him as He guides you personally. Return and reestablish your faith back into your life. To walk like Christ, you must also surrender your free will to God.

These are real facts of life, and they are all a part of the realities of this life of being Human! In Heaven Angels of God follow protocols that needed to be followed up there, and God is expecting nothing less from us down here on Earth! For so long, you have complicated your life with the wrong priorities that, you have lost tract of the wisdom of the real truth behind the facts of your life and your essence of being a Human Being created in the image and likeness of God!

So it is time now to let go of such ignorance and prepare to learn the truth and learn to live a real life! Living in too much ignorance will definitely deter the growth of your Spirit for God. But it is all up to you, surrender to God everything that you do, because the more you question and apply Science to try to figure it out, the more confused you will become! God and faith with God, is above and beyond neither Religion nor Science that ever have existed on this Planet!

Stop and think for a moment, trace back your life and reassess what you have done to your own existence first. Do not worry about anything or anybody else.

Your priority is always yourself first. Then your personal relationship with God should be first and foremost in your life.

Whatever happens to other people's personal relationships with God are their very own responsibilities not yours. Never judge others as you cannot judge yourself. In the end of our time, God will judge us uniquely and personally.

If you are hungry initially, then do not even attempt to feed anybody outside of yourself. You need to work on yourself to fill you up first, before you can take care of other people. After all, a hungry mother cannot just feed other hungry children of other mothers. Let God guide you through your daily life first in your surrender. Trust that He will fulfill His every promise to you!

He will even think for you and carry you when you cannot do it anymore. After all your hard work God will start working in your life. He will notice and will start paying attention to you! He will bless you right away with all the things that you may need at the time. It will be a beautiful new beginning for you.

You will start to feel the change of the course of your life for the better! Your heart will warm up to God again and you will begin to appreciate those little miracles that are happening around you! And you will begin to be grateful for the positive changes that are happening before your very eyes and deeply believe that everything that is of God is always beautiful!

Your misconception that it will be a scary experience is a lie from believing so much from the wrong source! Your pure heart and spirit will start to manifest itself with the gift of discernment by The Holy Spirit!

Then God will send His messengers when you are ready! The Messengers are also as important as the messages they carry for you. Believe in them, and then discern them properly with the help of the **Discernment of the Holy Ghost that is revealed thru this book.** When they come with messages that are filled with the love and lights from God, it is from God!

Anything that is coming from God is never about darkness, arrogance and hatred. If you have received any messages that deviates from God's good intentions and God's nature otherwise and is out of the context of Love and lights, it is not of God's.

It is always your responsibility to discern it properly as part of your training and Spiritual growth.

Here are the Eternal Tools of Physical and Spiritual cleansing and sacrifices:
A. Fasting, as a way to clean a stained spiritual opening.

If you have not tried fasting in your entire life, (and for health reasons it will be hard for you, please pray for your answers and consult a medical practitioner for advise.) As for me, I will tell you exactly the way I was asked to fast by my messenger Angel, St Michael. (On the other hand, you may not have him as your messenger, and again they will only come to you when you are ready.) Remember that in this book, I am only recounting to you the exact revelation of my deep Spiritual and Mystical encounters with God and His messengers as my personal experience. Your experience in the future may not be like mine's.

I am sharing this with you to help you in your search for God. My instructions were to fast two (2) straight days and two straight days of prayers and meditation with only small white cracker a day and a lot of water in a crystal glass without any ice.

I was asked to fast on December 22 till the eve of Christmas, which was December 24. (Please note that your personal experience that you may receive may be different than my personal instructions and experience).

Please take note also that I was told by Jesus Christ himself saying, **"Follow all instructions by heart, for everyday of fasting, a small piece of cracker a day, for two days. It has to be eaten only in a time when you most desperately need it!"** I was not allowed to sleep at all, until the sunrays go through my window in the morning of the next day. I was instructed to pray for every minute and for every waking hour of the night and day for those two days of fasting.

I was not allowed to close my eyes no matter how hard it is to stay awake, for according to St. Michael; the Devil can control my thoughts. I was also requested to limit my stay outside of my bedroom. I remembered St Michael told me one particular time and he said, **"Outside of your protected room, will not be as safe"**. I was also instructed to make an **Altar,** a place where I can pray properly and center my prayers to God.

I did make the required altar: a little place where I prayed so hard in front of my bed. I place a small table, cover it with white cloth, I then placed a blessed cross in the middle of the table, have holy water handy and a picture of the Holy Family and a prayer book that I continually read and use for praying for all those two days of fasting. I was then instructed to place a cross to any crevices and openings and doors and windows etc. (For your sake as well as for mine,)

Please remember that it was revealed to me that **fasting is a very important sacrifice that must be made in the cleansing of a Soul to mature into a Spirit of God and there is no other way to go around it. So fasting is imperative at that time for me!**

Like you, at this time, you might question why all the rituals? I did the same, out of being a skeptic. I never believed at that time that these are all happening to me! As I have said earlier though, when God is ready to touch you, whether you are ready or not is not anymore an option for you at that moment, but God's.

You may receive a different option for you but for me at that time, it was a sacrifice that I was not ready to make but I was told to make, and that proper fasting is imperative!

When the Physical body is weak, the Spiritual part of us becomes stronger to receive any Spiritual message, and it is easier to receive anything of a spiritual encounter that may happen. You will become sensitive to the spiritual presence, if you are spiritually in tune during the process of proper fasting and prayers.

In fasting, we relinquish control of our will and our resistance to give or to take. So we have to make sure that we also prepare a proper venue. It is almost an **initial Surrender and Humility at play** at that particular moment of time and experience!

A beautiful surrender indeed that can only be achieved if God is in the midst of it all! The serious side of fasting is to know that there is an existing danger of another encounter that may also happen that may not be of God's and His Messengers.

This is the reason why we must properly discern every encounter, every communication, and each and every message that come to us during fasting. When you fast, you must create a safe and peaceful haven for this sacrificial offering and ask God and His Angels for protection always. **Fasting, as I have understood at that time, must only be done properly and in only God's time and His Protection at all times.** Otherwise, It will be very dangerous when you are not strong enough Spiritually, as you cannot discern properly, and you do not have God on your side to protect you! The reason for it is because during the time that we are weak the Devil will also take the opportunity to take advantage of such weakness! So you will be in danger of a lot of messages that will only confuse and deceive you that may not be coming from God also! With proper fasting, you must pray to God, pray and pray for all the time that you are fasting!

Ask God to protect you from evil and asks Him to send His powerful Angels to protect you! During your sacrifice of fasting, offer your pains, tears, sorrows and joys to God! Everything that was your past, your present and your future, let

Him own it! And ultimately put your whole life in His Loving Hands in total surrender to be with Him!

B. Cleanse your Mind and Thoughts

Cleanse your minds and thoughts of all the negativism that have played in the major part of your living life. Get rid of it! A spiritual cleansing will not be complete without checking the powerful mental progress and the master and teacher of our actions, our Mind. Our mind can receive all the stimulants from the Universe, but the proper discernment, can only be expanded by the wisdom of your Spirit!

Our thoughts may it be bad or good will continue to evolve, depending on where we stand with our relationship with one another, and in how we live our lives for God! Our morals, values and virtues are all dependent on the degree of maturity especially in our Spirits.

Having attained the depth of our wisdom of life is really dependent on how God has rewarded our very own efforts, to live our lives the right way! The difference will be in gauging our true spiritual maturity. Without the proper use of our God given gift of free will, it will be an understatement to presume that we can hurt each other because of the powerful control of our minds! So be prepared to be educated with the wisdom that is only coming from God.

Make the right start in this journey with God, and make known to Him your true intentions and commitment. Without such, you will only begin a meaningless journey! Be conscious of how powerfully the Dark side can also deceive you by the way your mind and thought works in every aspect of your life. Be very vigilant of the way you handle your everyday life, as well as how you deal with other people in your life. Do not hurt other children of God! The merits that you will earn are coming from the difference that you made in other people's lives.

The mind, when working in the wrong direction can either make you or destroy you! Be vigilant, and strive for the peace that will calm your Spirit to free your mind of all its misgivings. Stand firm in your daily walk. Do not waiver in your faith!

So avoid and stay away from the unnecessary noise in your life that will only confuse your mind to make the proper judgment in walking your life. Start with a little pause from life and pray for God's peace to rule your life!

Be open to His grace of peace and be humble to accept your inequities! Let go of that Pride and exercise Profound Humility always. Then grow your Spirits to expand and receive the most valuable wisdom from God.

C. Maintain a pure Heart.
Second to your Mind is the Heart. When in pain your Heart could be in danger of being compromised in its judgment. The importance of how you wear your heart will play a major part in your active Agape life. The heart will continually give out the emotional energy to balance your everyday life. And this is the energy that will revolve around your life for as long as you live. **God will have more room to work inside a pure and Innocent Heart than inside an Arrogant Heart!** True love can be felt inside of a pure and innocent heart than in a lost, arrogant, and cold heart! The Heart is the most sensitive part of our Being Humans.

This World that we have lived in worked on energy always! May it be a negative or the positive one, you have the option. It is a choice that you will have to make and an option that is always open when you are ready. So use your freewill in the righteous manner and guard the health of your heart always! Safeguard and protect it from harms way. There is no telling how it can be hurt as easily and quickly in a daily basis. It will just react as you tread in the difficulties of life and in the way that you live your life! So take good care of the health of your Heart.

A Happy heart will make a Happy Disposition, and A Pure Heart is a good partner to your Spiritual growth. It is in this partnership that we must be careful not to distort. Keep the health of your heart. Preserve the health of your Heart and believe in the dictates of your heart, for it is where God lives within us if given the chance to rule our lives!

D. Go outside of yourself and your family to share Love.
You can never give enough love. The entire World needs love because many of us are not giving nor sharing it.

Love is a valuable and abundant commodity that is being horded by selfishness of the most people of this World. Love itself cannot survive when it is partnered with selfishness. Love has to be shared and it has to be also treasured! Love is the only ammunition that can be used to keep peace for all of mankind in this planet! Love has the spirit of selflessness that could surely be one of the most powerful of the Eternal Tools to heal this ailing World. And Love's energy will give it the light to drive away the darkness from our sight!

E. Finally the last but not the least, and is a very important must do for cleansing, is to PRAY, PRAY and to say more PRAYERS.
Know the proper way of praying through your hands and body and learn what to include in your prayers. The best way to pray, (as part of my personal revelation and for your benefit to

know) is to bow down your head, bend your knees and kneel before God's presence (honor Him deeply and in reverence in your heart) open your hands, palms facing up, and humble yourself before God. Empty yourself to God. Show humility with the feeling of total emptiness and lowliness.

Start by giving your message of appreciation and gratitude to God. Give Him thanks for all the blessings that He showers you in your life. Apologize for all your misgivings and disobedience in life. Ask forgiveness for your inequities and arrogance towards Him, and His other children.

Recognize your faults. Ask Him to help you live a better life and ask for His wisdom to make the right decisions. Praise Him for all the good things that He has done for you and for the whole World. Put Him in reverence, honor and Love Him most of all.

Empty yourself totally and offer you past, present and future to God and ultimately put you life on his hands and the lives of those people that you care deeply and all who are close to your heart. Give God your commitment to turn your life away from your sins and apologize to Him from the evil deeds that you have done to the rest of His children!

Honor, praise and love Him, with all of your heart and life! Make Him know that He is first and foremost in your life from now till the end of time! This time, you give Him all the credit that He so deserved. Acknowledge His continued support, protection and love for you. Feel special as a humble servant and child.

Let Him know now that this time ever in your life, you have believed in your self to be His best Servant and Child! Let Him know that He is finally welcomed in your life! And you are ready for Him.

Ask him to send His Holy Spirit to touch your life, your friends and the people that you love. Ask Him for the Eternal Protection of your life and call His help and guidance, to lead you back to the center of your life!

Pray for the light and love to finally inhabit this World and ultimately pray for God's energy to rule this World that you have lived in, and for the rest of your remaining life!

Chapter 2

The True Surrender

My Penitence, My Life!

After a while that I was gone...I wanted to return...
Return to the Center of my once long lost Life!
I drifted so long, and been gone forever, as I have recalled my selfish self!
It is I, why bother?
It is You, why care?
I am in control!
Forget the Deal!
It is too late to return now...I have been waiting for a change.
I have abandoned all cares...
God, please guide me again, I pray...
Please guide me to have faith and help me to surrender to your Mercy!
My aching Heart is tired...Thank you Go for all your Love!

Relinquish all control of your lives to God's hands! Let Him lead the way to your eternal salvation! He is the Creator and Savior of this World and He will come again to claim us back. The sooner we do it, the better it is for all of us! Be the Spirit for God in total surrender! Let go of your arrogance and your pride and open the door of your heart to accept the state of Profound Humility! Let your humble Spirit dominate the energy of this World. Life will be simple and in God's grace always, if this could be at all possible!

In the future, the Spirit will realize that it couldn't just exist by itself on its own mountain of pride, but in a partnership with its Maker. Welcome back God and reestablish your perfect personal relationship with Him.

God can help us grow our spirits since God is its Maker. Our spirits also knew deep down that there will come a time, when things will have to go back where it came from, our Spirits will eventually return mature or not! When the proper order of things and nature will fall into its place, God will require not less than total surrender of all the things that He had created breathing or non-breathing to be returned to Him!

God has given all Angels and all Human Beings that He had created in His image and likeness a gift that He has promised not to intervene which is the gift of freewill; to do as we please, and to be able to make a choice to which path we will follow.

God hopes that we will always use freewill to do well and to do good things. He also hoped that we would always have good intentions in our hearts. This is allowed to nurture a soul to mature into a spirit to be with Him! Out of love, God will patiently wait for all the good things to manifest from all of Mankind. And He has been waiting since time eternal because we are very slow in our progress and commitment of surrender and trust in Him. How we are at the present time is all up to us individually.

How we direct ourselves and how we behave is not all coming from God. Our own actions are just a manifestation of how we make our choices and in how we use our inherent gifts of freewill based on our Spiritual maturity!

There were many moments in our lives that we blame God for our misgivings. Remember, that we have the tools to understand a little deeper now, that we are responsible for every action that we take in our daily lives, no matter how big or small it is! The truth is real and we have to use it.

We cannot continue to be proud of our ignorance! To have the wisdom and be a wiser human being is a better option in the end! Then hope for the future will be a brighter one for all!

True surrender does not only entail going with the flow in what others would want you to believe. What other people believe is irrelevant to our personal relationships with God. What you have to believe is that this special relationship is only between you and God. We cannot be living puppets to other people's beliefs, but we can respect them for it. Personally though, we must make a stand in our own personal faith journey and to stand by God's truth, to enable us to attain the elusive wisdom to guide us to the right direction of our lives!

Our spirit has the strength and the perseverance that is beyond any Human Physical Capability. And for this reason, we must be vigilant not to let it grow the wrong way and ultimately give it its untimely demise because of our negligence!

It is the inner strength of the Spirit that will keep you going no matter what the odds. It is also our very own Spirit that does not give up on us in the end.

Our very own spirit has not been filled for a long time. The hunger of your spirit will continue for as long as you disobey God! So let us all try to work harder to expand it, so we accommodate the vast knowledge of wisdom that it can accommodate from God.

When you were lost in your journey and when you cannot find the center of your life, you drag your Spirit with you. It has never abandoned you, even if you have left it behind to starve for the rest of your life. If you could have grown your Spirit and nurture it properly, it could have been the most powerful tool that you could have used, to venture into a most powerful walk on this World! **But it is not too late. God has given us another chance, by revealing His Secret in this book; using His Eternal Tools of Alignment!** You could still give your growing Spirit, Love as a partner, and a lot of prayers as its food! And off you will go, to a most wonderful and powerful journey of faith and glory with a very pleased Father in Heaven!

If the spirit does not mature properly, surrender can never be achieved in the right manner. The Spiritual Strength cannot just be dictated to obey. It is the most stubborn and most powerful part of our essence as a human being that could either make or break us. The Spirit is the higher self and it has to evolve and mature.

If the walk was wrong in all the directions of your life, the spirit will be the strongest at the end to disobey. So, maintain its health and make it strong only to obey God's commandments always! Only then can God dwell in it as you walk our daily walks of life! Without the right spiritual growth, the stagnation of your very own wisdom will be inevitable.

You will have a world of chaos, for then, it will be very hard to make the right decisions and to discern every event that will need to be assessed in your life. At this point in your life, discernment will not be fully achieved if you continue to ignore the rules of God. And it will be a very difficult sojourn of life! If you start to build your home amidst the chaos of this World, it does not matter how much you have accumulated materially, because you will still be discontented and dissatisfied! In the end of time, all these material things will rot before your very eyes!

It will be hard then to arrange your priorities in life, because every move that you will make will be a strain to your heart! And all because of an immature spirit! In the end, you will be living in disarray, because your own walk is astray! This will be a life of confusion and dissatisfaction and total emptiness to no end.

True surrender does not demand growth of the Spirit in an instant, but to urge the spirit to grow in peace with its environment. It will give itself the balance and homeostasis it needs to mature eventually. To start the walk to properly mature the spirit, we have to be reborn again, be an empty vessel for God to fill.

A new beginning will then unfold before us. We then can start to slowly experience God in our Hearts, our minds, our bodies, and in our souls. For everyday that we will live, we will become a totally new person for God. So the walk will be a fresh start every time! Let us begin now to walk the walk, let profound humility be our strength. Let us not anymore focus on our endless needs and wants, but satisfy our own individual Spiritual hunger with the way we live our lives and the prayers we feed our souls.

Channel all energy to change for positivism and surrender most of all, our free will to be used by God alone. Let's start putting our lives in His Hands, and place all our priorities in order. Most of all leave everything to God. Let Him freely direct us to the right directions of our lives. In the end, the walk will be simple, and an easier walk. Then at last, we can endure the tests of time to live our lives the right way! A new beginning indeed for the right vessel! Alas! Finally, we are found. We are not lost anymore. We are giving ourselves a chance to deal with lives head on and in the right track! God will always walk with us and He will always be there to pick up the pieces of our lost lives.

He loves us so much that no matter how we challenge His patience and disobey Him, He will still continue to watch over us and give us the chance to reform. God is never demanding or impatient. So crawl if you have to, to God's fold again!

God's impatience only lies in the fact that we do not have Eternal Time to make the necessary change.

And we have been too slow to respond to His call. We have deliberately been testing His love and patience for us. And He still waits for us up to this time. He only mandates to see us in the right direction guided by His Love and Lights and also in the way that we live and share our lives with other people in this World.

How we can help to create a miracle and make a difference is what's important to Him. It is not even a matter of what is important to Him but what is important to you. You come first in God's heart and surely you can do the same for Him! Now that He has revealed the simple secrets of aligning our life again, we should not delay our response and run to get the knowledge that will help the health of our very souls. Then, we can at least help our ailing Spirits to its health and maturity that God has desired for it to achieve.

God will work with you for your own good. In living your life, let God be the light to guide you to the right path. Follow Him blindly, He will never forsake you when you go through a very difficult journey in your of your life. He will never abandon you in the midst of your miseries.

God is Love and He will show you what real Love is. God's ever encompassing Love and Light will cloak and protect you always. He will not run short of showing you His loving mercy that has kept you in His fold for a long time.

Surrender to God ultimately is the ideal way of living life on this World. It will be a life of strength and a life where you will rule with your God-given wisdom. A Christ-Like walk indeed! It will be a life of an almost perfection on Earth, which can be attained only by a mature Spirit of God in a Human Being. Only then, you can realize the true essence of your very own existence.

Then, you will live a life of fulfillment and total satisfaction. You will be self-contained; all your questions will be non-existent. And you will have all the answers available for any problem that may come to your life! There will be no hidden agenda in the future World of the mature Spirit for God. **A World of peace will be restored. By then all work in unison with what has planned for all of us…total happiness and everlasting full life and in Oneness with God.**

Surrender to God in the future will be very hard to achieve for all of mankind. We are all born with imperfection and thrown into this imperfect World that we will be too scared to let anyone or anything meddle with our lives, not even God!

Man is made of an ego that is still very immature and controlling. His pride will not topple that easy. It will take too much bloodshed and wars to keep that ego satisfied for any man to change. And we have fallen because of this ignorance and deliberate arrogance!

There is so much ignorance and misconception going around. And to those who consider themselves Scientific and intelligent still continue to search God thru Science and end up always with little or no right answer! They have to smell, feel, touch and taste God before they will even believe that He has existed. They travel all over this World and the near Galaxies to prove their point to lead them ultimately to a pointless direction and distorted facts and thinking! War will also be the product with too much exercise of arrogance and pride on this Planet. We have become a cold shoulder to lean on even for our very own brothers and sisters in God!

Pride also contributed to our deliberate Spiritual downfall. And because wisdom was not gained properly, more questions will arise from a stagnated point of view. Ultimately we are led to the stagnated growth of the Human Spirit.

The problem to this is that, there will be no real answer for them or anybody for that matter, because God is a mystery that will take a lifetime of Spiritual Maturity to discern and God is above and beyond any advanced Science on this Earth!

If Earth is only a speck of dust in God's hand; surely God could have created a Galaxy far greater and far more scientific than this Galaxy. Another Galaxy could have existed within a Galaxy, and another within this Galaxy and to the end of time!

God as the Master of all Creations Has never stopped creating numerous! Planets and stars to prove simply surround us. And the truth is to have all the answers to our questions, is to gain back the wisdom from God!

It is man who is making it more complicated to see God. Surrender to God, and God's wisdom is the only answer available to Man at this time. Man complicates his life because of the wrong thinking and his immature spirit. What a man thinks is right for the moment will not be necessarily what is right by God's in the future of our justice to come on this Planet. So be aware and guard yourself from the eccentricity of your failed and deficient Human Nature. Be accepting of the truth, that only God is all knowing, because He has all the answers that you do not have. It is up to you to humble yourself and accept such inequities as part of your own creation! And then, ask God for guidance and to complete you.

I would encourage you now to put your guard down in the matter of your faith for God. Remember that we are now in the time where the signs are actually right in our face. Pay attention around your surroundings.

People change, time is changing, and the weather is also changing. The generation by itself is changing. The future is very uncertain and unstable. Feel your Spirit, feel your heart and reach your highest thought.

Can you feel something different in your life and this World's events? It is time to make a mature judgment. For the first time ever God is calling upon you. He reveals the secrets now on how to directly communicate with Him through Alignment.

In this book He has instructed you which tools to carry and which path to choose. This is the time now for a chance of establishing a lifetime relationship with God.

He is revealing to you where you can find Him. Deserve this chance and do your part to meet Him halfway! Do not question Him anymore, you are running out of time and the time is now. Be open to the change and look forward to your life the second time around. Accept the new beginning that will pave the way for your ultimate happiness in the end of time!

So close your eyes reach out and call Him, He is still there waiting for you to open up your Heart and your mind to give Him a chance to walk with you! Know that this time is right. Knock at His door but not too loud, He hears you so clear. Just remember though that this walk is only for the deserving. Come get prepared, use the tools and May God be with you on this journey!

The Almighty Power of Love has been ready to receive you in the glow of His warmth. He is counting on you to do your part. Show Him that this time you are ready to play your part and let your actions speak for itself!

The total embodiment of Love has come down from His Kingdom to honor you… so come honor Him and meet him halfway. Let the Spirit of God in you soar to the highest Heaven to embrace His love. Surrender your all in good time, for there will be no other time again to be called this way and so clearly.

"In due time…all will be surrendered to His name!"

Chapter 3

Mankind's Sacrifices

I needed You and You needed me Lord!
You have opened my eyes, now I can see!
You have opened my ears, now I can hear!
You have opened my Heart, now I can feel!
You have opened my mind, now I can think!
You have ultimately opened my Soul, now I have grown to You!
You have taught me the Spirit of Wisdom…
In loving, you have let me be!
As I needed you Lord, You have helped me!
In my time of plea, You have rescued me!
As I hurt you Lord, You have forgiven me!
Thank you for Loving Me!
I now knew that as I have needed You, You have also needed me Lord!

If for eternity God has sacrificed for mankind and even gave us His only Begotten Son to absolve all our sins and to redeem us from our inequities and sins, surely all of mankind must be pure and deserving of such a sacrifice from God Himself to come down and communicate to us at this present time and in our own very low level. God's Love for all of mankind was always so unconditional, that He has spared us all from our untimely demise and He has continually protected us from the darkness of this World. The only problem that we may encounter at this time and in this generation is that now, we have forgotten that although he created the bridge thru Jesus dying in the cross to give us a purity deserving of Him, a chance to be reborn in this manner does come with a little price that we have to pay.

I said a "little price" because our individual price is to just to live our life to the utmost and be a responsible Human Being. To be deserving of our inherent right as a human being is another thing. We must follow and obey God without question! We are judged ultimately for the total way of how we live our lives on this stage, called Earth. It is without question that we have to ask God for forgiveness for our sins as we continue to live our lives in disobedience and disarray. As we are not perfect, He does not expect you to be perfect in everything that you do.

As the saying goes, "to err is human, but to forgive is divine" is very true in this case. We can always be forgiven if we repent and by asking for personal forgiveness from God, when we do make a mistake. In the real walk for God, there is indeed some degree of expectations from us. We all must be responsible for anything that we do big or small in this World. We have to be responsible not just to ourselves but also to other people around us, may it be our families or our friends.

Always remember that in God's eyes your merits are not always based on what you do to yourself and your family, because it is already a given fact that you will take care of yourself first, and then your immediate family, but also what you do outside to make a difference to the other children of God. The merits that we receive are not mostly based on what we do for ourselves. The heavier merit is based on how we make a difference in other people's lives, aside from how we live our lives.

In the servitude for God, there will be no more egos and self-centeredness. In order to serve God properly, the Humble Servant must understand that he or she does not exist for him or herself anymore, but only exist to serve his true master, who is God and His children. If we have to use the tools above that I have mentioned. We will soon realize that we cannot afford to make a mistake without taking any responsibility for any of our actions. For in the end, we will reap what we sow. A better harvest is expected from a good plant. It can happen, and it is not impossible. That's not assuming that you will understand me of course!

If you are not Spiritually growing, and you continue your wrong practice, there will be no other person that you are going to hurt in the end but only yourself. Let's get to where I am getting at. Let's answer some concerns and questions you may have. Is God saying abandon all and come follow me means that you must leave everything, your material wealth, and your family, and then start starving yourself and at the end, live in the jungle with the animals and be eaten later on by a big crocodile? My dear innocent man, the answer to this question is a big no!

God will never wish suffering or damnation to all his children that He loves so much. To wish you suffering through the abandonment of your material possessions is a pure and blatant misconception. It only means that if you can maintain all your riches in this World, and can be beyond being greedy to the rest of hi other children. God wishes that you could still be selfless even with all the riches in the world. That even if you live in your Golden Palace, you can you still unlock your door and open your heart to a dirty, thirsty and hungry beggar, who knocks at your door!

It is not the matter of how much you have, but the richness in your Spirit of Love that you can go beyond your material possessions to help another Human Being in need. God does not want you to focus on the material and to put a price tag to your every action of kindness, but to be the real hero of your time, to spread goodness and mercy no matter where you are and what you have. If the situation is reversed and you are very poor in the material accumulation, you are still God's most loved son or daughter. Trust that he will add things unto you and bless you with whatever you need at that time. What will matter most for you is to know that, your Spirit is full and balanced. In the future, you will be strong in your quest for survival no matter what the odds are because you possess a Strong Spirit.

To sacrifice for God does not only mean material abandonment, but also to defer in the satisfaction of the need for greed in the Mind, the Body and in the Spirit for ones selfish motivation and fill the Spirit this time, with the real food which are in the form of good deeds and a lot of prayers! We can let go of our wants and needs if it is not a matter of life and death situation. If it is not like the air that we need to breath to sustain our lives, we can let it go of the rest of the unnecessary trivialities!

The Sacrifices must be pure and our Intentions right. It is imperative that we heed only to listen to the truth and not to color code our choices. In Heaven, the rules are either black or white there is no such thing as brown. If you have chosen otherwise, and choose brown, be very responsible and ask forgiveness to continue the bridge in your walk with God. Humbly know that as sinners, we will continue to displease Him, because of our inherent imperfections. If at a certain time, we may make brown as our choice, just knowing and accepting our faults in profound humility, will help us to redeem ourselves later.

God has given us endless chances and He will keep His door open for us, if we will continue to maintain the bridge between us and Him by repenting, and turning away from our sinful ways and by asking forgiveness. A change is needed at this time of our lives. We have to change for the better. If we have continued to hurt other people, we have to stop now. We need to know that only we can change our individual selves. Where you stand is your responsibility and what you do and how you play your role in the stage of life will be judged later on and we have to be vigilant at all times to guard all our actions and intentions.

God himself will not judge you by how other people will judge you. In the end of your life, He will ultimately judge you, based on how you are in relation to other people. Only God has the right to make a judgment on any breathing and non-breathing

Creations of His. So make a stand. Do not mind what other people will say about you. **Live according to the right principles by God and worry about your relationship with Him first.** In the end, this is the relationship that will matter most in your whole life. And ultimately, it will be your personal responsibility! Only you, can save yourself with God's help!

Do not be confident that just because Jesus has died in the cross to save you, you will not do anything else to change your wrong doings, because you are already saved. This is a misconception that will distort the right thinking! It is very dangerous to preach this kind of misconception to other people, because you will take away a lot of people from God's side. It is not correct to think this way. This is a very dangerous way of thinking! Jesus death on the cross to absolve all men of their sins that he did not commit himself is just another chance for redemption that God has given us, out of His love for all of us.

The Heavenly Father has given us a fresh chance, and a fresh start, in a pure and an unstained Spirit, by giving us His only Begotten son because of His love for all of us! This is the only way we can reestablish our personal relationship again with God, after we buried ourselves in the filth of our sins. And then we can proceed to continue our lives, with a clean start!

Every time that you have disobeyed God's commandments, every time that you hurt other people, you are still expected to make amends, repent, be responsible, and to change your ways to save your lowly soul! When you disobey God in the way that you live your life, or in any way you deal with His other children, you will still have the responsibility to make amends with Him on the wrong doings and the harm that you have done. God has always expected you to be a responsible Human being with your daily walks in life.

Ignorance in the above case is not an excuse! You will unconsciously cut the bridge between you and God, by not being conscious of your responsibilities. You have to be responsible for all your actions, and also to ask forgiveness and pardon for all your wrong doings in this planet. Ultimately your sins as I have stated previously will seek you out from your hiding place. No matter where you are going to hide, your sins will ultimately find you. It might not be paid at this time, but it will be paid in God's perfect time! To reestablish the bridge of communication between you and God, you have to know that there is no running away from responsibility.

So take good charge of your life and be very vigilant of your actions! Without taking the responsibility, you will grow stagnated in your Spiritual growth. Part of your reality is to be pardoned for your sins. You must always ask forgiveness to purify your soul in your everyday walk with life! If by now you do not understand me, please pray and ask God to communicate to you in the language that you can understand! The wisdom will come to you to help you understand in the future. My dear friends, after He purifies you, you will still have the responsibility to keep that purity intact, than to readily stain it in a daily basis. For if you believe otherwise, you cut the bridge that binds you with God. As you offer your sacrifices, do not sacrifice for the sake of sacrifice, but do it only out of your love for God.

God hears your true intentions said or unsaid. Walk clear of any wrong intentions always. Start right with God and ultimately end right by Him. Communicate only the purest of the pure in your intentions to Him. For the present time, sometimes it takes Mother Nature to remind us to remember God during times when we become helpless. It takes a strong calamity to utter the words "Help me God". It is because we are so focused in the way we have lived in our high and mighty pedestal. And when we are high up there, we feel very invincible.

It is the pride and arrogance of the way of our lives that make us forget our lowly beginnings. Nothing will happen to us, we are so proud to admit even to our very own insecurities. We convince ourselves that our money can erase all the pain and all of our sufferings later on. Then we get so busy with our pursuit for the accumulation of everything that is material. Again we forgot sacrifice, love and honesty and we also forgot to surrender to the truth to God's wisdom!

The present time that we are in, we are actually in the time that God will want us to experience the truth of our true existence and He will make sure that we are also reminded to pay heed to our responsibilities. The truth will be hard and the price will be high in the coming future of this Planet. Weather will change and survival will be very hard for each and every one of us. If Earth is pregnant it is due for a big transformation. And the signs of the time that I am talking about are already before your very eyes! Actually, we are really overdue for a Big Transformation.

The revelation that was allowed for me to peek in the near future of this World was very real before my very eyes. And then the events that followed after all these years just confirmed it for me. And I had no more doubts for the rest that is about to come and happen to my lifetime! Let me remind you that God has a good plan for you. In that plan you must be ready. He is still giving you the chance so take it now. Start your life by welcoming Him back into your life! Mankind will be forced to sacrifice in the future, if they are not doing it already.

We will be hastened to our own punishment for the wrong doings that we have not repented. God will side with the lowly that gave their all to Him. He will topple the high and the mighty that has hurt his other children. Our sacrifices in God's eye will not be based on whether we do it now or later. Can we get away from it? We may or we may not, only God knows!

Sacrifice is part of our existence. In life we sacrifice for our loved ones. In our careers, we sacrificed our time to be productive members of our society. We do a lot of sacrificing to bridge that gap of our responsibilities and ourselves. With God, it is not sacrifice for the sake of sacrifice, but to take responsibility for our actions, may it be big or small! With God, we are expected to give Him love back, as He loved us.

It might not entail a lot of sacrifices from our part, but it requires us to be conscious of our relationship with Him. If you disobey Him, repent and ask forgiveness! If you hurt His other children, apologize and take responsibility. We must not point our blame to the stars to avoid taking responsibility for our actions. And above all be humble in front of Him and in all your dealings with your fellowmen.

Take heed that this is the time to grow our Spiritual selves and gain the Spiritual strength to aid us fight the battles of life itself! With a strong Spirit, there will be no more excuses. You will be taking charge of your life this time and in the way that is only righteous, and in only the way that God has expected you to do. You will clean your every action of evil and will only follow God's lead to live a righteous life! Remember that you cannot just hide from the misgivings that you have done in the past. It will be a misconception, that just because no one is looking, you can get away with your wrongdoings.

With God, you cannot hide. In the end, your sins will seek you out. You may not pay it at this time, but your family will in the end, if it is not you. So be conscious not to give the bad karma to your loved ones.

As you grow with the knowledge of being a true Christian and with the wisdom that God will ultimately bestow upon you, be wary of believing in the lies of this World to confuse you. You are your own responsibility! Be vigilant of your own Spiritual health at all times. I am just showing you how they have showed me.

You may or you may not believe me…but I urge you to listen to your heart. With proper discernment, you will understand me in the future!

Jesus said to me one time, **"Beware of non-believers, but do not worry, I know my flock, they will heed your words without resistance. And for those non-believers, move on there are so many more lives to touch and so many more souls to save".**

When I heard it, it gave me the strength to reveal these things to you because Jesus also promised me that He would touch you through this Book. I hope that at this point of reading this particular page, you have a little discernment to believe that God is internally working His miracles inside your individual Spirits. Close your eyes, listen to your hearts, and feel Him! Now, I am only relating to you my personal encounters with God and his messengers. I am not willing to compromise the purity of my experience by adding or taking away the gist of the entire experience. Like you, I also have the responsibility to obey and only write the truth of my experiences. I cannot afford to be disloyal to God, and I cannot afford to make a mistake by Him. I will tell it to you as to how it really happen as it happened.

Your experience later on may not be totally very different from mine. How you will gage the success or the failure of your experiences will vary again on how God will bless you with the wisdom that is only given to your growing spirit. Most of the time, my experience communicating with God comes in the form of conversations of some kind of parables that are communicated to me. The information was always given to me in a piece meal method. I am not given all the information at any given particular time. Most of the time, the messages are symbolic.

When I look back now, I have understood that at this point of my Spiritual growth, the wisdom was so vast and could overwhelm my entire Physical and Spiritual existence. If all the information that I have received could have been given to me at the same time, I would have to die my whole Physical body first and then have to receive the messages in the form of my Spirit. Only my Spirit will be able to expand to accommodate the infinite wisdom from God.

And also because only my Spirit can expand and can accommodate such enormous amount of information and wisdom! Most of the information requires some urgency to act upon it. Sometimes it is about this World but sometimes, it is about other Worlds, mostly though, it is about the Celestial Existence of Heaven, or perhaps a Paradise that is only intended only for my eyes and for your eyes in comparison to the future of this Planet

Chapter 4

The Sharing of True Love

"Oh LOVE... You can make me or break me! You came knocking at my door to visit me. Gladly, I wanted you to stay. To stay with me! But you are such an illusion and I got my demotion. Now, you've left me... Oh Love please be true to me!"

In this worldly existence of ours, we sometimes get confused between what Love really is, and as to what it symbolizes for in our lives. We keep searching for its true meaning in our lives. We searched so hard to figure it out. Is it a feeling or is it just a state of mind? We just go on and on in this limbo of trying to understand what can make it real for us and for our lives. Is it from the mind, or is it in the Heart?

Love is such an elusive thing and maybe an illusive dream to understand. And at the present time, how we really know what love is a matter of how we truly think what it is! No one really can give out a definite answer to our infinite questions on the meaning of love. We like to think that we have experienced love at least in some point of our time, but we never really think deeper if there are other kinds of love that holds more meaning to our lives!

We kind of got stuck with the wrong notions of love, as we have gone astray from its deeper meaning in our lives. Physical love dominates our Materialistic Earthly life more than ever before! Off we go just as innocent as we can get. Because we truly do not know what part is love's role-playing in our lives that we run away from, because to most of us, love can hurt! We are scared by Love that we have refused to give it the commitment that it needs to survive. After a while, lost and lost we go to loneliness, confusion, desperation, and aloneness with any kind of love being absent from our lives. We fall face down sometimes when we are face to face with Love! We have refused the responsibility and the commitment for Love for so long, that we cannot carry Love the right way in our Hearts! But wait a minute now! Let's figure it out together. What if we try to feel love in our Hearts and then let our Minds experience it too, will this be a little easier to discern by our mature Spirits?

If there is a harmonious co-existence of Mind, Heart and Spirit, it is possible that true discernment of real Love could truly be experienced at last! My dear friends, what I am trying to tell you is that love could come from different forms and from different places in our lives.

It could also come to us when we least expect it! Ready or not it will affect lives whether we like it or not. Sometimes we confused love only in the form of our Physical and Romantic lives. It is understandable that although we have focused our lives on what it is right now, in our personal relationship, we got lost somehow in the deeper understanding of how true Love really is in this romantic relationship!

True love in a romantic relationship will play a vital role of establishing a harmonious partnership with another individual, because it is a relationship that is not selfish or arrogant. It is both the Spirit and the Mind in its true partnership with each other that will lead such relationship to the level that is blessed with understanding and kindness.

Love in its true sense will create a very supportive and harmonious relationship with each individual involved, because it is not just based solely on the Physical, but also the Spiritual level of the relationship. Love will then have a higher level of feelings and emotions. The experience of a true and profound romantic love will be just a matter of time in a given relationship if true feelings are involved. There will be depth in this kind of relationship. It will be a peaceful coexistent of a man and a woman in Love.

The so-called "soul mate" will then be achieved and learned the right way. In the future, shallow relationships, will then be replaced by committed and lasting ones. Happy couples will abound in the true Spirit of partnership with God! God is the total embodiment of love itself!

When God is present in any Love relationship, it will be a lasting one! Sharing of true love on this planet, can only be realized when both the spirit and the mind mature to receive God's wisdom and apply it on each and every relationship of life on this planet. Even if you have attained the highest education that any man on this Planet can teach you, it will not guarantee you the highest wisdom about Love that only God can give you! Come down from your high chair and humble before Him.

Accept your inequities and God will surely bless you and fill up your empty vessel. The rest is up to you and God.

God will bless you with all the wisdom that you can accommodate. He will be there to guide you when you are lost with your search for anything. With God, everything on this planet is possible! Strive to learn the proper way to discern things. Let your Spirit guide you. Ask God to make decisions with you when in doubt and leave everything in His Hands. You are favored in His Heart for God has always loved you!

Where does discernment come from and who does the discerning? The only answer is that part within us that has the most powerful gift of discernment and wisdom from God - The mature Spirit of course! A mere immature Spirit within you will not be able to expand and accommodate the vast knowledge of what God will bless you! Make it expand to learn the wisdom of the Universe! You need to grow your spirit. In God's Spirit, you will be full and not hungry. The Spiritual food is not of this Earth! Remember to fill your Spiritual void with prayers and more prayers! If anything else fails, including your physical body, your Spirit will live forever to be with God.

Be worthy to be welcomed into His Heavenly kingdom! Start your sojourn in the way of the Lord. Love is the answer to this ailing World. Heal this World with the light of your Love. Do your part, and God will do the rest! At this point in your life, remember that your mental capacity is too limited to accommodate God's wisdom and truth! No matter how scientific you think you are, you are just a plain Human, and very limited to all that God can bless you. I do not want to put you down in your place, but this is the simple fact of your life that until now, you have refused to accept. If you are not humbled, God cannot work on you.

"All that welcomed Him, by faith...must surrender to
Him, God who is
Almighty in Heaven!"

Your arrogance will deter God to work in you. Because He is not welcome in your faith, He will not force Himself in for you. You have to meet Him halfway! He will not come to you if He is not welcome! If you have been paying attention to what the few pages of this book have unraveled, there will be no question in your mind as to what your answer is going to be.

You must let God use your will and you must surrender to Him to lead your life! **Everything in this Book is weaving a tapestry of answers and revelations from The Eternal Tools of Alignment that will teach you how to be truly gifted with the real gifts of wisdom from God! But a little work is required of you and you must do it. There is no reason for you to make any more excuses to take responsibility of your life and its direction. Have faith and believe in yourself and in God.**

In this chapter of love, Love is a very important ingredient of life, because this is the only ammunition that God has revealed that is a must to carry in our every day's journey with life. Love in any form, must not be abused. It is an Eternal gift from God, to give you depth and substance in your journey with life.

This is a gift that He gave to us that could come in many faces and we must be aware of it. It is His Love Divine that He gave us. It is true Love that He wants from us. Let's learn how to discern the right Love to give Him, and to give to our different relationships on this planet. He deserves it and we all deserve good Love. In the end, God will give us back His loving ways tenfold in our lives! This is not the kind of love that we carry most in our lives, for we mistake and abuse love in so many ways.

We have also misrepresented love in so many ways because of our misconception about its meaning to our lives. We are still very much confused about the meaning of true love in our own lives. We are also still lost in our journey with this gift called Love. Like our essence as a Real Human Being with the mature Spirit for God, Love has to evolve into its highest level in our lives to go with our mature Spirits and loving relationships.

As we grow our Spirits, Love will also grow. As we mature, it will also mature with us. When we have a relationship in the end, we would be able to share our one true Love in the way that our mature Spirits have discerned.

With The Eternal Tools of Alignment, it is easier for us now. God has revealed the secrets to His loving ways. We are given the chance to relive our lives away from evil. This is the time when He truly shows that He cares for us!

God has given us a way to redirect the center of our lives. As His faithful children, it is our duty and our obligation to obey. As I have mentioned previously, if we can properly mature in our Spirits, there will be no more questions, only answers. As we grow, Love will too! Life will be a good adventure to experience the second time around as we share God's true Love.

True love can only be experienced and not just wished to us and to other people also. To experience true love is to be almost as one in the Spirit with your Creator. True love will go beyond its boundaries of time and of space. True love paired with a mature Spirit is like an almost perfected achievement of faith and relationship in a Human Being. A Human Being who is also full of love also for God! In your baby steps of aligning yourself with God, using the Eternal Tools, along the way, you will experience the pain of growing up. It is okay, it is allowed.

Life is the best teacher and God is your greatest Professor, so you are in good hands! Without experiencing pain, you will not be able to really appreciate happiness isn't it? When the road is narrow, the journey in the end is worth it! A wider road does not guarantee the right path when more options open up.

Choices have to be made and then you will lose your way when so many roads open before you. But with God's guidance, you will never lose your chance again for your salvation and protection! Begin to appreciate the innate tools within you and within your reach. God has prepared you for the trip. His only wish is for you to have to end your journey to His Eternity of Love that is waiting for you in Heaven.

Share true love with each other. You can, and you will discern properly now. God has given you the gift already, by just reading this Book, because this is His Book!

If you have managed to finish the first Book…you are now enlisted in his army as one of His loving soldiers. The warrior for God has no hidden agenda. He is working only according to God's will. Above it all, know that you are being watched by Heaven and protected by the Heavenly Angels.

You will be favored and will not be hurt anymore by the pains of this World. You will endure this World and you will be stronger the second time around! True love mandates a lot of sacrifices that are yet to be made. In the reality of our most difficult journey of life, True Love will make us endure the tests of time. The sojourn will be very painful sometimes but will be bittersweet in the end. When love is used as ammunition to make a difference in someone's life, a happy relationship of peace and warmth can be achieved as this World revolves around energy. At this time, love's energy will revolve around this World! True love when felt, will make a person complete.

He will lose all that unnecessary insecurity. He will begin to notice his or her value as a Human Being. He will regain the strength to start believing in himself as well as other people in his life. He will be making a more meaningful journey in his life the second time around, and he will be inspired to live his life again!

There will be no more unnecessary noise and no more unnecessary paying attention to trivial details. People will be communicating more with their hearts and their minds together. Reasons and feelings will go hand in hand and true happiness without selfishness will dwell in this World again! Without selfishness, true love will slowly be realized.

It is a hopeful possibility in the future, if we adhere to listen to God at this point in our lives. Let us start by redirecting our focus to the main reason of the essence of our existence, and to obey our Heavenly Father. It is without question that somehow God has lost us into the darkness of our lives.

The unfortunate abyss that we have created in this life has led us to our own eminent destruction! It is selfishness that will destroy True Love's good intentions in our lives! Our meaningless existence will continue if we are not careful. In this World, true love can be possible if given the chance. And this time is the right time for all of us to answer as God is personally calling us to go back to His fold! Let us be free again from the bondage of the darkness that has engulfed our very own flickering lights.

Love has to grow with the freedom to be able to initiate its flight to its highest height. To cage Love will only deter the light that is about to shine so bright upon this World; for Love is a part of the Universe of Light, and it is the aid and the companion of wisdom that is intended for each and everyone of us to attain. The absence of love would only mean total darkness in our lives! The presence of God's light in our midst is because love exists in our lives. The reason for love's absence is when we lost God and we also lost true love in our lives!

We cannot imagine having God's presence without love, for God is Love, and Love is God! True love is never selfish. It has a sacrificing trait that when felt properly can be an invincible strength to remove your mountains of pain and a very good tool to guide your life in the matters of the heart and in the matters of your own personal happiness. Love can be felt within your heart. It is innate within each one of us. If it is true love you want, work on it in your life and start your journey with the God of love!

Unfortunately, in this lifetime, an ignorant, selfish, mean, and immature Spirit of a man can endlessly abuse love. Man in his high pedestal will refuse to surrender to love because he is scared to relinquish control of his high and mighty chair to somebody or anybody. Because of this, wisdom was not attained. Man by nature is comfortable in his restless life. You cannot really force any man to come down from his high and mighty pride. His decision will be his own.

For a selfish man, any emotion is no emotion. He'd rather sulk in a corner than care for this World. It will be a grand task to change this man to become a normal Spirit for God. This man's World is chaos and his life is a very noisy one.

He also thrives in this kind of environment because he is determined for self-destruction. He is unaware of the light and is not so suspicious of the dark. He will depend on misjudgment, as he is easy to judge. Use true Love as a tool to walk this Earth. Make love be one of your precious possessions. Guide your life in the light and warmth of love.

Let it cloak your cold heart from the storms. Make yourself an example of true warmth and care. Let the rain in the storm be cleansing your life. Gather your only ammunition that is love. Spread it as far as the endless Universe. Believe in its power and soak yourself in its Light! Remember all the good times of sharing love. Let love create those precious memories and gather its beads to weave your unforgettable moments.

The unforgettable moments of Love will last forever, for forever is a trait of Love. Love always weaves those interesting colors of life. Life itself will lose its meaning without love. Imagine this dark road leading to your path of disillusionment in black and white without the colors of love in your life! A lifeless existence of unforgiving sadness, and weary heart in a land of discontent! Ah Love…it is not my journey, but yours to tread.

Let love be our guide when we make the choices. Let it be shared when we walk hand in hand in our united search for happiness. Let love's powerful energy be the torch of our lives!

Let love fulfill its destiny in your heart. Let it be home with you in your stand for a more fulfilled life, and let the future holds its true meaning in your life through Love!

"When all things will fail…Love will always remain!"

Chapter 5

The Preparation of your True Dwelling

"The Bridge of Life"

The bridge of life is like a shadow in the mists of Avalon.
It is like paradise, in the clouds lined with Gold!
The bridge of life is where the Chariots of God passes by, to the True Dwelling in the sky!
True Dwelling of Love!
True Dwelling of Lights!
Eternal Wand of Peace and Eternal Life of Bliss!
"In the matter of your faith journey for God, the true dwelling does not lie in the making of a place of abode in the middle of a bridge. It will be senseless to try to explain the existing dwelling in the middle of a very unstable place. But this is sometimes how we apply our lives on this stage of life, called Earth."

    The same dwelling cannot be made as a permanent place of residence. It is so shaky and so unstable. It is also just a temporary stage of our life! This is an unfortunate product of our faulted focus that has continually led us to our own destruction and we do not even know it! Our way of life has turn to nothing as to what God expects of us. If we do not listen now, when the Time for Transformation will come, we will be in God's mercy! And it will be too late then. So let us begin to open ourselves and receive the truth of God's wisdom in our lives!

    This Planet called Earth is only a stage. This Earthly Plane is a very temporary stage of life. How we really play our roles are really up to us. We must not be ignorant to start building a permanent place of residence on this temporary stage.

    We are just passers by on this stage and can be removed anytime whether we like it or not. Know that God is the builder of this stage and He will take it away from us again in a matter of a heartbeat, if He wills it to disappear!

    The true awareness from the wisdom that we have gained is vital to our way of living on this stage called life! We must be vigilant and be obedient to God's rules and His voice.

We must answer every call that He makes. We are privileged to be His children but by any means, we do not have the right to abuse such privileges! The stage of life is allowed to test us on how we use our God given gift of freewill. It is a gift that God Himself promised not to intervene with our use of it! The gift of freewill is an essential tool that can be used either way in the direction of good and evil. The existence of good and evil in our lives are also allowed to be able to teach us the lessons of life. During those times in your life, that you have blamed God for your own misgivings, it was not really God's doing, it was your wrong use of your gift of freewill. Be honest with yourself, God loves you so much that He allows you to exercise your freedom to do whatever you want with His gift. Along the way, you hurt yourself because of your own ignorance, not God's!

God is all knowing and ignorance is never a part of God. So be careful and take responsibility for all your actions. Understand that although you have the gift of freewill, you are also expected to exercise good judgment. Be obedient and be open to the words of wisdom because it is also useless to baby-sit a man who refuses to listen and to learn a new way. God will continue to follow a blind path of self-destruction that will be ultimately inevitable. Avoid being that man! It is useless to argue the truth of your existence! Man is very stubborn for his own good.

Live according to the commandments of God not according to your backward morality. In the future, it is you who will be responsible to answer for yourself! What matters most at this time of your learning is that, you are ready to commit yourself now to God. Although it is a hard reality for now in your immature Spirit and understanding, it could be a possible future for all of us if we are willing to change! The truth sometimes hurt, and this is one of them! We always try to avoid the work of our Spirits because it is a reality that we are never really are ready to accept or understand. We naturally avoid the issues that we cannot control or be able to comprehend. We are so comfortable in our own comfort zone that it is very hard to change.

It is always easier to escape from the reality that takes so much work to do. As we do our things differently, we deviate ourselves from the center that we are supposed to follow somehow, and then we follow an empty path to the nowhere land. We cannot continue living like this anymore. The signs of time are afoot! We cannot continue to be blind, and be blinded by the wrong moralities of life. Each careful step that we take will earn us some wisdom in future of our lives! So let's welcome the change.

If you have to choose now, would you rather have an easier time in knowing the truth? Or would you rather swim in your ignorance to avoid taking responsibility for your life? Having to work your life in the style of oblivion is like getting lost in the middle of an ocean of frustrations. Lost and lost we go to the point of no return. So this time, come let's journey together and extend our hands to God waiting for us to receive and welcome Him back in our lives! Make Him feel all worth the efforts that we are about to undertake, to change our lives!

Let God take the lead and make your commitment. It is especially helpful now that we must really be conscious of every move that we have to make each day of our life. The reason for living is easier to understand if we start right from the very beginning every day and getting the wisdom and learning it every step of the way. Compare how we could have lived our lives living with God and to experience God in the midst of everything that we do. Compare the happiness that could have been, living in a Paradise called Earth and a World without an end!

Would it matter to you if it were possible to achieve? Would it change your views about God, God's love, and God's existence as real? Your stand with regards to these matters is your own private views. Only you can make the change to change yourself. But always remember, that with wisdom, you can have all the answers that you also seek. In the end, you will experience God and change your life for the better. You will see the light of day, and the change that could transform your life into a beautiful adventure of a love journey!

To understand your total involvement right now as we go in this Book is paramount in making your decisions. It is imperative that you practice to give a little commitment to something even if you are not used to. To continue this journey of life and learning the ways of the Lord, you must open yourself and hang on to your faith. Your faith is beyond any religion. It is not a matter of practicing your religion anymore, that you will be judged in the end. What matter is how you practice your faith!

Your faith is your very personal relationship with God. How you humble yourself before Him and how you obey Him will matter most! In the end, only you will be responsible for your own self! And you will have to answer yourself to Him. Whatever is your religion right now is immaterial to your salvation and wisdom. It is easier to talk the talk, but it will be even harder to walk the walk.

So, are you walking what you are preaching? Be honest with yourself. I personally will say to you, that I will humbly acknowledge how imperfect I am. And I will humbly admit that I will never attain the perfection on this planet in my whole lifetime, because I was already born with the imperfection since the day of my conception. With God's grace and blessings, He will guide me to grow my spirit with the wisdom and the peace that will help me in dealing with my life and my faith! I know that deep in my heart, my love for Him will also be the force that will make Him notice my humble existence and my growing spirit! Although

I was given the privilege to peek a little bit of Heaven and see God's glory in action, up to this time, I am still a baby, just like you, in the middle of this vast knowledge of wisdom still waiting to be learned. I am still walking my baby steps in this lifetime, and to share a little glimpse of what I have seen, is still very worth the try, because of the beautiful impact it has given my very own soul and my personal journey with life! Stumbling will always be a part of my learning and my walk, because that is how imperfect I am. As I grow, I am wishing for most people of this World to grow with me.

My only wish is for you to believe that God truly exists, and that He will give you a little peek of Heaven as He did for me. In the future, you will be rewarded the wisdom that is just right for you! I am glad that I was given this chance to share with you. And I am also glad, that I could share with you something beautiful. Deep in my heart, I truly wish for you to experience God, because it is the most beautiful adventure that you will ever experience in this lifetime! I am also glad that that I was given the chance to be skeptical about everything that happened to me, and to be able to get the wisdom of understanding from the Holy Spirit, that was there working continually to give me the wisdom to understand.

I am hoping that this Book will become an instrument in your life that you will carry if confronted with obstacles as you tread a hard path. It is my fervent hope that the burden that you carry will be lighter, and your life will be easier with the use of the **Eternal Tools of Alignment with God!**

Your real dwelling is not on this World. This will not last. This is temporary. This World that you live in is only a stage to play your role. Play it well and deserve yourself a better life and dwelling in the future. Somewhere out there is where your real life really begins, your true dwelling and your real family, is out there waiting for you. So is your Eternal Father! In the newly established Paradise on Earth, you will dwell in total awe and happiness.

It will be a Paradise that you have never experienced before. An experience and a true journey that will give you exhilarating ride to the top of your perfect satisfaction of life itself!

The colors and the materials of this place are made of crystal. There is a golden highway in the sky! You will adorn this place by your mere light and presence. The ornament in this place is not based on the quality and the quantity of the decorations put into place, but by the Celestial and Ethereal inhabitants who lived inside and the lights that shines from their spiritual presence.

The grandeur is not on the display of any ornaments because there are only but a few, but by how the Celestial Beings adorn the place by their mere presence of love and lights! Floating in the grandeur of love, off your spirits will glow in the dark with them at your side! This could be a future reality for you. Hard to comprehend as it is, there will be no comparison on the grandeur of Heaven's Kingdom in comparison to any kingdom and any experience of royalty on this planet.

There will be no comparison in the grandeur and in the light that will emanate from this new World and Paradise! But it is very real and it does exist somewhere in the future of this World, when God will ultimately come in His full glory! The pastel colors will be pleasant to your eyes and the weather perfect. No need of needing anymore, because there's no more to need.

There will be no more wants, as the need for wanting will disappear into thin air. God Himself will provide for everything! This is a perfect place that none could be compared to it! Believe and secure your place in God's Kingdom. As you obey His commandments now, your questions will be answered by the wisdom that He will bless you later. Work your way to His Heart and He will be there waiting for you! Carry that true faith that will pave the way to His light! In this lifetime please pay attention to where you are going. Anticipate living and enjoying the next place of perfect dwelling that is waiting for you.

Pay heed where you are going. Temptations are going to be present and will always be a part of your life on this planet to deter your walk. Ask God and His Heavenly Angels for guidance and Spiritual strength when you are lost! Remind yourself that this is just your temporal life on Earth. You are just a passer by and you will soon leave this place to be at your real life in God's Kingdom. There is such a thing and believe in it!

It will benefit your growing soul to start to embrace such an elusive reality for you. It is not a dream. It is very real. God's spiritual kingdom is at elbow's length than your own physical World. It is very close and it is real!

You are on your way! Come celebrate. This time you are really given a little peek of Heaven. The true and real dwelling that is always there waiting for you. The reality of its existence will be revealed to you in good time. The manner in which to achieve it will depend on your strength to pursue it. A good place, in a perfect time and in a perfect space has been always there. It is up to you to open your eyes now and see for yourself!

Your new knowledge of God's reality should always inspire you in whatever it is that you have to do. Achieve what you think is impossible, because it is. The possibility of this reality is right there before your very eyes! Train your heart and your mind to simplify your direction with the help from the Heavens above. Be cautious of the means and the ways that will deter you from reaching your destiny. Redirect your faulted focus back to God again. You shape your own future and you will reach your destiny in good time.

The path is laid before you. Take advantage and learn the facts of life! It is easier for you than it was for me, knowing you were given this book and I was given the crash course before I was even ready! Believe me when I tell you that reading this book and learning from it is easier, than walking with it straight and learning from God and His messengers directly. It was an awkward walk of faith that I could never even begin to imagine that it could happen to me in such an opportune time! When God will seek you out, ready or not, you will be amazed by the speed of wisdom that will be poured unto you. I do not know how much you can take it, but I will tell you this, mine was too much to last me a whole lifetime of Eternity of Life! Embrace this new knowledge. It will help you understand your faith deeply. It will also give you a chance for God, if you did not believe in Him at first. Christians and non-Christians will be given a new breath of the life and love that the Heavenly Father blesses this World.

Be righteous in your walk and make the right choices. God has chosen you to be made in His image and likeness and surely we only have one Eternal and Heavenly Father. Regardless of your race, color, religion, status, and cultural orientation, we are all coming from the same source of our lives, from the Heavenly Father that created this Planet and all of its inhabitants!

Simplify your life with this knowledge, and walk and treat other people that are around you, as your own brothers and sisters. Do not continue your walk of ignorance of hatred towards your own kind. Give love to heal this World from all hatred and pain of persecution.

For Christians, Jesus said,

"I do not need your prayers, pray directly to my Heavenly Father, He is your Father that is in so much grief, for your people have hurt Him for a long time."

Then he continued saying,

"My death in the cross, to redeem you from all the sins that I did not commit and out of my love for you and my Father, has no meaning anymore, and for most of this generation, because you Humans continue to sin against my Father without asking forgiveness for all the wrong doings that you have done continually."

This could have been a good message for you to understand that when you are teaching other people about being a Christian, you must also learn how to repent and turn away from your sins. Just because Jesus have died for you to redeem your sins and give you a fresh start in life, you are still expected to keep that sanctity of your Spirits through your good actions always and to repent and ask forgiveness for all your wrong doings.

It is very dangerous to teach other Christians to continue to sin and get away with it, because Jesus has already saved you! By doing so, you will be taking more people away from God from this misconception. Be a responsible teacher, and do not allow yourself to be an instrument to teach the wrong teachings of the dark side! If unclear, pray for your answers and be strong to listen only to the righteous teachings of God! Rejoice and be happy with the good news for it is just a start of a good beginning in your life.

Be vigilant and refuse to fall into the abyss of lies and corruption of your soul. Start the journey of your life in the total commitment to yourself and to the Lord. You are His most favored child in all of Eternity. A walk with God in your true dwelling is like a walk of fame and fortune that is beyond this world of broken dreams. Pack up your things and prepare for a journey to your true dwelling. This journey is the most interesting walk that you will ever make in your life. The true kingdom is not far away but start your journey early.

God loves you and He will be joining you soon. Do not lose your hope and your faith in Him. Trust Him always with every step that you have to make in your life! In the Lord everything is possible. Live in the positive light and God will dwell forever in your life. Let His love manifest in your life and start anew with a journey to a full Spirit of God!

"In God the Father we trust, In Christ the King we have recognized the unity of all of mankind!"

Convey the good messages of God's love to those who need it. God loves you no matter what! There is no question of His love for us when He has sent us His only begotten son to die on the cross to redeem us from all of our sins! And God loves all of His children on this Planet. This is only one way to show us His unconditional love! Stay in the fold that will differentiate you from his non-obedient children in the End Times. Life is good with the Lord. Be a warrior for Him and stand by Him at all times. He is all that you need to endure this lifetime!

Dwelling in this temporal life is not an easy one. Make it easy by putting your life in God's hands. In God the Father we trust. Let him guide you to the quickest way to follow your path towards your dwelling with Him. Let it be your lesson that total surrender is needed in finding your direction and in making your way to His heart. It is not in how you accumulate your tools to pave the way, but in how you use its finest and simple qualities to help you find your way to God's Heavenly Kingdom. God's Heaven only exists in the simple dictates of your heart. When you have a pure heart, God will dwell inside.

On Earth, your Heaven is God's Heaven too. Your success is his success and your failure is also His. To imagine a World without Him would only mean a total emptiness of human existence without the light and the wisdom of God's love. This World that you have lived in is just a stage where you are tested in how you live your life. This is a stage of life where you are tested with the tests of Human endurance and of Human survival. It is without question that living a life without the Heavenly Father is a life of nothingness that will ultimately lead us to our ultimate destruction of despair and frustrations. A life without guidance from God, will lead us to human pride that is our very worst enemy and which is not of God's character.

When our existence is based on the not so godly undertakings, our lives will be doomed to its utmost imperfection and utter destruction and our world will be in total chaos.

Remember to respect your body as a physical sanctuary of the Holy Spirit. Be prepared to accept the serenity of your World to accommodate the peace that your spirit will need to be inhabited by the pronounced sanctity of your own body. Your true dwelling will encompass that which is you and your surroundings.

Your actions and your behavior will have a great effect on your Spiritual growth. Do not waste your time in learning the trivial matters in life. Focus your direction in the direction of truth and wisdom from God!

The tendency to outwit any Spiritual growth during the process of learning, with the excuses of inconsistency, will only destroy your already stained life existence.

If your soul will stagnate in its growth to be a growing Spirit, it will not hold a life of maturity for God! You will truly end up in despair in the future. A risk that you should refuse to take! Prepare yourself to move into your true dwelling at all times and be ready to move with the speed of the wind and listen to the dictates of God's own Heart!

Rejoice at the knowledge that is revealed in this book for you to use. Remember to live each day to the fullest, as if it were your last day. Be ready for God at all times…you will never know what each day has in store for you. Without a strong faith to begin with and without some aid to help us like the Eternal Tools of Alignment With God, life will be harder to deal with. Our own realities will be distorted to nothingness and emptiness. Our walk will be slow and painful and our quest for God will be endless!

There will be no depth and true understandings of the nature of things of this World. There won't be any meaning to the facts of life, and we will be spiritually lifeless in our sojourn and in our quest for God! At this point in your life, it is time now to profit from the knowledge that you will learn from this book.

These are God's messages before your very eyes. Feel Him in your heart calling you to respond to His call. Lift you heart up and anticipate the coming of God in your life now and in your future! The Kingdom of God is out there waiting for you. You are very special and are especially loved for all of eternity!

With open arms, our Heavenly Father is waiting for you in the true Kingdom that only you deserved. Remember that this Kingdom is not in this material World that you have created, but in the Heavens up above!

In the future, when all thing swill settle down by God, He will descend on Earth in full glory, and He will show you His paradise that will be reestablished again on this Planet! A World with no end where He will ultimately live amongst us!

A Crystal Palace in the sky!
"I saw the sky opened, looking up, I saw a Crystal Palace seated on the clouds of dark blue and the lightest of gold, lined the Superhighways of the sky, then I saw Jesus in white robe, in the middle of the garden of beautiful flowers inside this Crystal Palace in the sky, and in the future, He will live amongst men!"

Chapter 6

The Merits of Living Your Life for Others

"Rewards of the Healthy Spirit"

The difference between you and me is not about your way or mine...it is the difference that you take to show!
In the hearts of the people around ...tears of glee for you!
Without you.... sadness and fear!
You have helped unburdened the pains and sorrows of their tomorrows!
You guide them in from darkness and you shed them from their foes!
Your wonderful actions say that you have provided the light aglow!
You have never wasted, wasted your time for you.
Heaven will reward you as Heaven is for You!

God has revealed that the lessons in life are not based on how you have accomplished your own destiny with all the successes that is humanly possible in your whole lifetime, but in the achievement of such good destiny thru the most people in your life. It is helping one soul at a time, to grow into a Spirit for God.

Your own life is not just a reflection of what you have done, but a reflection of what you have done for others in your life. That is how we are judged and in how we play our role in this temporal life! And most of all, how in God's name you have unburdened the sufferings of other people than your own! This realization will dawn upon you automatically as God will continue to pour into you His wisdom of truth. It will be a hard walk at first, for the changes will happen to you when you least expect it.

In the true change of living for others, you have already surrendered your precious will to be used by God! As God used you as His instrument to spread love and good deeds, you will grow to understand that you do not exist anymore for yourself but you are now living for the sake of other people in your life!

The harder the walk, the deeper the wisdom learned. Making a difference in other people's life is in God's eyes the most important part of your mission on this World. It is a selfless mission of existence and living the will of God. It could be a very hard work for most of us, because we are used to the comfort of escape from our responsibilities for a long time. To go back and retrace our step is the hardest way as we are as scared to face the truth sometimes. When you live for the sake of other people, although it is one of the first learning that will be given to us, we are also expected to be aware of the balance that we need to establish with our relationships with other people in our lives. This balance is imperative in anchoring our stability and decision-making in the future.

Sometimes when we get too serious with the mission, and because of our limited understanding, we might mistakenly interpret the meaning of selfless existence as totally forgetting one's self and our personal responsibilities in exchange for other people's responsibilities. If you have to think this way, you are already not balanced in your own action.

God only wants to use the strength of your Spirit in discerning the wisdom of this lesson and in spreading His words the right way. He also expects you to learn not to take His words literally! This is mission that will not be possibly accomplished in time, without the proper understanding of the meaning of your ultimate goals in life and without understanding you true essence as a human being. The balance of your Spiritual work will depend of course on how much wisdom you receive and how much work you have placed in your Spiritual growth. You have to take the time to examine within yourself, what areas in your life that you will have to redirect in the position of goodness and righteousness for God. As I have stated before in this book, you cannot just go around the preparation of your physical and your spiritual vessel the right way, without using the tools of **God's Eternal Tools Of Alignment**. You have got to do it!

Refresh yourself from these teachings and learn from it. Besides living a life of selflessness and profound humility, you are also expected to make the necessary sacrifices and the good deeds that He requires of you! God cannot start the work for you when you lack the basic understanding of His basic rules of alignment. Another factor is to understand that in order for you to receive God properly is for you to prepare a very clean vessel for Him to fill it up. You will not be ready to receive Him in the condition that you are right now, in a stained Spiritual vessel. Cleansing is imperative even before you can start your beginning journey!

In total surrender to God and as a follower and a humble servant and child of God, you do not exist anymore for your own self, but for others. Living a life for the sake of other people, and taking care of others needs other than your own needs first. In the future of your life, you will find more meaning in the value and in the purpose of your life.

It is of living out of a selfless motivation rather than a more personal selfish motivation, because selfishness will be a character not known in God's nature. If all human existence will be based on this selfless practice of life, life itself will be evolved into the right direction of its original purpose of oneness, unity and love for all of mankind.

Goodness will rule in this planet and love will be the guiding energy of light for others to follow! The true meaning of living for the sake of others and practice living it in your lifetime will give each and everyone of us, the enlightenment for the right reason to live life properly and will give the human Spirit the value of its Earthly existence.

The need to evolve the spirit to be mature is vital in maintaining the health of a soul, who is in a mission and servitude for God! Understanding in how you live your life properly will bless your total existence with the right wisdom to rule this World. Your spiritual strength is the force that will be powerful enough to accommodate the vast wisdom of knowledge from God.

For then your success will not be based on yourself alone and only in your personal accomplishment, but based on how you made a difference to help save any one soul at a time. Saving one soul at a time will get God's attention to your work as His favored and obedient child. It will be too deep for a stagnated soul who is not growing properly to understand this wisdom, for we live in a very selfish and very material World. But in due time lessons will be learned and lives will change for the better!

Material things and God have an inverse relationship. Until a higher spiritual growth can be achieved, deeper understanding can be attained in the future. Very selfish Human Beings indeed that cannot handle the truth about goodness surround us. This will make the growing a little bit painful and a little bit harder. In this lifetime, some truth will carry with it some degree of pain. But the wisdom that is only coming from God will protect us from the lies. Although material things matter to us more in our daily practice of life, for survival in this planet, this accumulation of things on Earth is somewhat immaterial to God. The house you lived in, the cars you drive, the material wealth that you have accumulated for a long time, will not guarantee to save you and protect you from your spiritual self destruction and death!

In the end, these things will rot first! What really matters most to God is your Spiritual maturity! Cure your ailing spirit of harmful irritants that will slowly starve it to a destination of a lifeless existence! Choose to grow it in the level of being a worthy cause. Give it the direction of light and love for a start. Nurture the growth with the holiness that it deserved for a long time. If everything else will fail, God will claim it to be seated with Him in His Kingdom. What we may think that really matters to us so much, is what matters to the Lord, may not really what matters to Him. Paying so much attention to the trivial matters in life has made us forget what will really matter to God in the end.

Material possessions and accumulation as your life's goal will only push us lower from the ultimate growth of Spiritual maturity if we are not careful. I am warning you again that too much material possession will not really matter to God, as much as it matters to us. As long as you do not have the balanced growth in the spirit and has not attained the wisdom yet, anything that you will do will be ultimately in question someday. But when you do the right things, you can feel safe within yourself and you can actually pay attention to the right details of your life.

In your life, always question the wrong things and live your life the right way. Avoid doing the things that will hurt other children of God. When you start wrong, you will always end up wrong. In helping, the more you help, and the more you make a difference to the other people of God, the more merits you will get in God's eyes. The merits that you and I will be rewarded are our very important mission in our lives and we really have to work hard for it. We, as children of God must work hard to deserve God's attention again.

The merits that we will earn in the future, is not a direct manifestation of our personal achievements but rather a direct result of our personal work of selfless intervention in other people's lives.

So we have to be aware that God sees everything that we do, and it is hopeless to lie our way from Him. It will be of utmost importance that this wisdom of living for the sake of others must be thought of in a well-balanced perspective, along with the proper dissemination of the teachings of God as you follow the path of your faith journey.

Do not subject yourself to fall prey to conceit and to deceit of teaching the wrong things to other people. Do not judge other people as to their way of life, because God is the only one who can judge anybody in the end! Let other people grow in their own time and at their own pace.

When you teach, remember that your mission is only to guide them to God's direction. If they are non-believers, leave them with love in their own pace and time.

Jesus said to me one time in one of my visions with him, **"When you spread the words of my Father in Heaven, remember that I know my flock, they will listen to you without resistance, but for those people who are non-believers, do not waste your energy, leave them with love to learn on their own pace and time and go forward, there are many more souls to save in your World!"**

Just to look back from the above teachings from Jesus himself, has made me realized that this World has a lot of stubborn children of God and it will be very difficult to even try to change anyone's view or anything else for that matter. Living the right way or walking the right walk, is a very difficult way, because it will involve some personal sacrifices and selflessness that we might not be used to for a long time. Just talking about it will not suffice the expectations that are laid before us to follow from God! And it will not be complete without the deeper understanding of a mature Spirit who has attained the wisdom from the word of God.

It might be a mystery to you that your walk is not just your own anymore. In your shadow, lies the beneficiary of your actions in this lifetime. Your merits are not counted in your immediate presence but also from your past and you near future of loving not only yourself but also other people in your life. So make your everyday walk count to earn more of God's merits. Maintain a healthy Spirit at all times.

Do not worry too much about your imperfections, as God already know who you are more than you know yourself! Remember that after all the grief that you have given Him... He still loves you!

Always understand that no matter how good you think you are, there are still other people who are a lot better than you are; in different degrees and directions of their lives. By being in another person's shoes sometimes will help you understand that even you are not alone in your confusion. There are more or less worst people, depending on how you give such importance to your own reality of existence. You are what you are made of and the difference will be based on the actions of your Spirit always!

Once you exist for others and walk the walk of how your very own Master and Savior Jesus exists for you, it will be easy to understand the workings of a true Holy Spirit walk for God!

You will indeed experience the special strengths and visions that only God can provide for you. And you will become gifted beyond your human comprehension.

Treasure these gifts and guard it with your life! God needs you as His partner on this Planet. Give Him every moment and all the time of the day when He calls on you. Spend your time with Him and be ready always to drop everything that you are doing, when He calls you! Be strong and do not waiver in your faith in Him. Believe in Him and have faith. Walk with the confidence that you are always aware of your limitations and strengths. He already knows your imperfections. Understand that the stronger that you are in the spirit the better it is for your life! Remember that God will judge you not from how good as an achiever that you are in this material World, but from how good you live your life for the sake of other people other than yourself, in the eyes of God!

Pay attention to other people making numerous sacrifices for you without any expectations because they have the right reasons for doing so. They have grown to love you unconditionally, because they have always applied God's love in their lives! In the future, you can always repay them with kindness that is not coming from your material acquisitions but from your priceless love and honest concern that you have for all humanity.

Make your humanitarian action offered only to the main source of your life that is God and your Father in Heaven! Have the right reasons and good intentions only in your heart, mind and in your spirit.

Finally, strive to earn God's trust. It is very important that He sees your commitment and spiritual strength. There will always be expectations and standards to maintain the health of a growing Spirit!

Chapter 7
The Exercise of Profound Humility

"Humility At Its Best"

On bended knees you have been praised!
I have praised your Love at peace!
Your happiness glow...in happy memories anew!
You walk with nothingness and....
Made friends with Emptiness!
In humble praises your heart sings, the way to God's commands!
You are not faint in your Humility, as God has crowned you worthy!
In humility you go, as a Humble Servant should know...
You are rich in memories, for your God loves you!

It is without saying that Humility is a very important ingredient in the proper walk with the Heavenly Father. Aside from Love, Profound humility is one of the most powerful tools to use if we have to work our way to get closer to God's Heart.

By emptying our ways from the dark stain of life, we can readily prepare our vessel spiritually from the arrogance of our past behaviors! For God to work in you and with you, you must empty and rid yourself of conceit and self-centeredness! When you are half filled with such degradation, there will be no space left for Him to be accommodated.

God does not go where He is not wanted and welcomed. It is unfair to expect Him to go down too low in your level and to demand His immediate attention, if you are not honestly really ready for Him. You have to put the light back into your life.

Your blatant disregard and disrespect for God will not work in your favor. It plainly won't just work, not in your lifetime, and not on this Planet! The selfish demand and the arrogance of any Human Being will never get God to pay attention to him or to her! It is not God's will to be absent from your life. It is because of your ignorance and stubbornness to change your ways that he was not allowed to work in your life! You need to make a decision to change, because you need to be saved from yourself! In the end, you will have to ultimately come down from your high and mighty pedestal, to meet God in the bottom of your humble state.

And you will be wiser to prepare for that time now! Any show of arrogance and pride is not of God's nature. It is not of His nature to show you boldly, how much power He has to impress you. You knew better than that! It is your duty, to come down and empty yourself from the dark corner that you hid yourself for so long. God will surely meet you anytime, anyplace, and anywhere. Do not be impatient with your wait. You have let Him wait for you for all of eternity to even begin to listen to His voice calling you. Start your journey with God as clean as possible. Begin right by Him and you will end up right with Him. Choose the right path and follow His lead. God will see to it that when you are calling Him, He will be ready to work on you and bless you. Ultimately, He will want you to empty yourself in profound humility, so that He can add more things unto you.

Please do not waste your time, start with an empty self already so you can accommodate His eternal blessings from the very beginning of your sojourn. Believe in His power of love to guide your daily walk. Follow his lead and you will not regret.

Every move that you will make, He will always be there to protect you. Follow your heart for he is there somewhere in the purity of its actions.

With humility in your heart, God can have an easier walk with you. Without humility, He cannot just work on you. Also understand that Humility is not a weakness in God's eye; it is a strength. Meanwhile without it, Pride will take over your Heart that which is really your weakness, in God's eyes. When pride takes over your walk on this World, God will be absent in your life for He is not welcomed in your Heart. Pride will open the door to your own despair and abandonment. Do not get fooled and be aware of your daily walks in life. The walk of pride is not the ideal walk. It is not of God's nature.

Be aware of the confusion that accompanies your weaknesses. You will be misled sometimes, but go back and retrace your steps and correct it. Slowly but surely, pay attention to every walk that you have to take. This Material World that we lived in, is full of Pride and Prejudices. We have walked too long in our ignorance and in our failure to surrender to our very own Creator and God. Because of our very own misgivings in life, our circumstances may differ and our wisdom and spiritual growth are definitely growing into its stagnated state. Without the wisdom that we can gain from God's blessings, life will be a harsh and difficult reality for all! It is not God's fault at all that we have surrendered to our very own ignorance for the wrong reasons. Pride will surely destroy the good path of our direct communication with God.

Pride and arrogance are ever partnered with the devil. It is love and humility that will partner with God to lead us straight to His direction. Pride and arrogance will eventually disappear in our practice of life, if we continue to avoid falling prey to the claws of darkness. It will be a hopeful journey for the future of this Planet. Pride will harden our hearts and will make us cold. It will blind us from the true realities of life and its true wisdom. So, do not subject yourself to the pretences and to the superficialities of life where pride can come in at any time to disturb your already peaceful life!

God and Love will walk hand in hand versus Pride and the Devil Himself. So if you really examine both Worlds of Existence, you can have a more realistic Choice. Whatever choice you will have to make is an option that is always be open to you. Remember that when in doubt, always pray for your answers from God directly. Knock at His door and it will be opened for you.

My questions for you will be where are you going and what are your choices? Until you make a choice to go back in goodness and in the light, you will be walking in an uncertain path to a walk perhaps of destruction and ultimate demise of your Spirit.

The wisdom and the virtues in life have been here and have been established for you from the wise of the old. There is no measure as to any evidence of what is right and wrong in our choices. It is up to God to judge us, but we must be conscious of how we walk and in how we live our lives. The rules in Heaven are either black or white. In this life, to adhere to God's rules, is to learn of God's truth always. There is no room for excuses.

If imperfection were to blame for Human weakness, it is also in God's mercy that we will be forgiven by Him, if we only humble ourselves and repent before Him.

Humility is the greatest strength of any human spirit at work with the Spirit of God. Man can start the journey at an opportune time of redemption for himself from his own sins with God. And with humility, anything in God's eye is possible for you. He can only work in you and with you, if you are humbled and lowly in your actions and you have accepted your inequities.

Just to humble and to recognize your own limitations will make God pay attention to you. In the time of your life that you even feel that you are not worthy, God will make you so, because He works in His perfect time for you!

Discernment will come to us by using our freewill properly and with the enlisted help and guidance of the Holy Spirit. The Holy Spirit of God will work in our lives if at the least we are humbled in our ways.

I am wishing to explain this information to you based on my Spiritual wisdom and growing Spirit as simple as I can explain. I cannot grow your own spirit for you, because you are your own responsibility. My mission is very consistent and it is only to show you the way.

I cannot pick up the broken pieces of your heart or the broken pieces of your life! Like you, I am just another humble servant and child of God too. I am not allowed the work that is beyond me to do. I cannot afford to make a mistake by Him. In the end, you will learn the wisdom that is given automatically to you when you are ready.

How much wisdom you can take, will again depend, on how much work you put into the growth of your spirit. Wisdom in itself is a lifetime experience that will take the whole Spiritual space of our Being. And the Virtues will only make it stronger.

How we apply it in our daily life is another matter and will take a lot of hard work from our part. We cannot always be consistent in our ways, but we can surely try our hardest. Be joyful in learning and knowing the secrets in how to attain a higher spiritual existence.

This is the day of your revelation. This book, will unveil the simple truth of God's ways for you to learn. By taking your time and by studying your life, you will know that the answer is just right there in your heart! As you go, remember that true wisdom cannot just be achieved only in some small walk that you are going to undertake. It is the product of your big steps also that will matter most in your quest for God.

Your dedication and honest commitment to your life righteously, will put you off to a start to have an experience of a loving relationship with God in your life, and will have a profound effect on the leap of your faith in the future! It will entail the whole big step in your walk, and the total dedication on your part, as you tread in your personal walk of faith for God. Wisdom is readily given to the ones that are ready and mature enough to receive their gifts, which are the gifts for the mature spirits.

The giving of ones self to other people in the highest form is to be in the practice of profound humility in living your life. God's absence in our lives will void all that we have worked for in our spiritual quest. Living a lie and a life without God is an empty direction of destiny itself. God's Kingdom is the ultimate direction where our Spirits will go back to share His Kingdom. When all things on this planet will start to rot and die, it is our mature Spirit that will always live forever to be with God!

This is a future reality that we have and that we must pay attention to. We have to upgrade our spiritual lifestyle in conformity with its ultimate mission, and that is…to live forever to be with God! Humility is one of the key factors that we have to practice in our daily life. Without a humbled spirit, it will be very hard for God and His messengers to even communicate with us. Although it is easier for us to fool our way into the masses and say we have been a humble servant, true humility can only make sense when it manifest itself through the other people that we have made a difference of. When Jesus died on the cross to redeem us from all of our sins, He has exercised profound humility in dying the way He died for all of us. He didn't use any magical powers to impress the whole World to make us believe that He is indeed the true Son of God. Jesus did not have a need to boast His position as the true and powerful King. He didn't need to.

God wanted to show us how He unconditionally loves us in total humility and lowliness to clean us out of our own filthy sins that He did not commit. He did it out of true love for all of us. And boy! How much He suffered for such a love! I hope that we really deserve it. He has exhibited true Love for all of mankind, and He has exhibited a very profound humility for us to follow! Just to remember the true example of humility of Jesus, the only begotten Son of God to die for us on the cross will remind us of our humble place on Earth. And let us remember the humble state, when He was born in a manger, around the animals in a very poor situation, where he was born in a very humble place, in a manger!

When it comes to luxurious accommodation that is fit for a King, He could have chosen it in a heartbeat, but no, He wanted to show to us that the way to His Father and our Heavenly Father is always to put our feet and be grounded on this Earth through profound humility!

As Pride has been very inconsiderate with our walk, so is the pain suffered by Humility itself. Make sure not to fall prey to the evil that is always lurking around the dark corners to take advantage of our spirits and are continually working, to deter our walk for God. So go ahead and march with the strength of the spirit that will only represent you as a true warrior and to serve only one God, who is your true Father in Heaven! The energy of ignorance and pride will ultimately succeed in our lives if we are not careful.

If we have become neglectful of our duties with our Lord, there will always be repercussions later on. But behold, it is not a matter of just preaching, but also in the matter of walking the right walk, that will matter most at the end of each of our journey of faith on this World.

Pride and selfishness have been the enemies of the past and the present. The ignorance and unforgivable self directed pity, which we have placed upon ourselves, would continue its way to our personal destruction. Our conscious ignorant minds will continue to overpower our Heart that has been crying for help for a long time. Our future heartaches and pains can be avoided in the future by learning to maintain a healthy heart this time, and also to keep up with the wisdom of a strong spirit!

We have been the long time notorious enemy of ourselves. Definitely we are our own worst critics at times. We have become very stubborn and disobedient for our own good.

This is because we wallow in our pride and arrogance for such a long time. We have refused to cede surrender to God's guidance and we have not gained the wisdom that we need to guide the future of our individual lives!

This annoyances of the past, is the Devil's lure to deter us from doing the right thing for God. The prince of darkness is so determined to keep us from God and His Heavenly Angels! He will keep on with his destructive nature to stop us from believing in God. He will try to displace God in our lives and to force us to connive with him in his conniving ways of eternal chaos and total destruction of mankind. But this is not the way to live your live.

Place the love and light around you in your walk with life again! God has and will always provide you with what you need and the protection that you will seek in times of troubles and obstacles in your life!

Be at peace and be in harmonious balance of your mind, body and spirit! It is the only way to keep a healthy relationship with God and all His Heavenly Celestial Beings and His Heavenly Messengers. Let us not be willing participants to walk with the Devil, but let us all walk with God. With our commitment to walk in the light of the Lord, be assured of a protected walk at all times in the future of our lives! It is our very own choice in life to listen to our pure hearts and what it truly dictates.

We are never forced to serve God nor forced to appreciate Him for all the loving mercy and blessings that He has showered in our own lives. If we start with the surrender of our prides and our egotistic ways, then God can then start holding our hands and walk us through the right directions of our lives.

Profound humility is one step ahead for us in the right direction. Without surrendering this part of us, God will have a hard time working his ways in our lives. Profound humility is a must and a very essential ingredient in our journey with God. In the everyday walk that we do, we must always remember to humble ourselves before God, our neighbors and to our World.

It is not hard to practice humility by starting it one day at a time in walking our daily lives. With the practice of humility, we can avoid to hurt people for pride will be at the back burners and will disappear ultimately like the boastful wind that it is.

We will then be able to make a big difference in our life and in the lives of our neighbors. Humility if allowed to work in our lives, will make us to mature and to be a better Spirit for God. Our lives will be easier and full of fulfillment.

If we have nothing but pride, we are just as much as an empty and hungry spirits for God. A fulfilled life will be reestablished in the whole of humanity again with this little changes that we can do within ourselves, one spirit at a time, and living it one day at a time. With a humble heart and spirit all will be harmonious in love and peace. We could be anticipating its peace and our love will be realized. Life will then be more meaningful, if lived in Peace and Love!

A humble life and spirit will be the strength of this World to come. The Spirit alone will be formidable against the wickedness of darkness. Its stronghold will be established eternally in the true strength that is only coming from God's blessings since our natural birth. We will surely exhibit this strength and God's nature and ways in our lives.

Love, peace and order will be reestablished again in this World. We cannot allow ourselves to be weak in this direction. How we practice our daily lives matter so much more in how our hungry spirits will receive what we are willing to feed it. Be conscious of your everyday walk and be very vigilant that you do not open your door to open the side that is so dark. Dread the fact that without God on your side now and in the future the Devil will take advantage of you any time he is given a chance.

Be vigilant that anything you do big or small will open the wrong door and will invite an uninvited guest that you will have a hard time eradicating out of your life later on.

Battle every temptation to make the wrong moves with humility to accept the right choices. Remember always that humility has never been a weakness but a true strength and a good eternal tool to help you in your sojourn to the right direction of your life! God's door will open for you. Receive Him in good spirit and in your own good time. Ask for God's true wisdom to help you in your journey with life on this Earth. If the roar of pride will disappear in this World, this Earthly place is still the beautiful haven for the marriage of Love and Peace.

Aim at having it replaced by the melody of your humility, and share the peace and love straight from God's heart to yours! So, be conscious of what you do always. Be very aware of hurting anyone with your words and actions. Be careful not to let pride play its role in your life. Your humility will balance your walk in the way of love for your fellowmen!

Pride will only complicate the matters in your everyday living and will not give you the peace and love that you have truly desired. Be aware and be vigilant of the lurking darkness in your heart. Let it out and open your heart to God's light and love to rule your Heart. Replace your selfishness to selflessness and start your kind acts toward yourself first and then to your neighbors next. Always start every journey with a strong faith that you are going to undertake your walk in the right direction.

Ask God, for the strength and the guidance in your daily walks of life. Go back when you are lost from the center of your life, and retrace your steps slowly back to God. Remember that starting wrong will always end up wrong. Do not expect to start wrong and end up to finish right. It will never happen!

Be conscious that the rules of our Heavenly Father are black or white, not brown. If you go brown, be responsible! That is a small thing to ask to help strengthen your spirit.

Come and let us start together in our baby steps and let us be humble to accept our true Destiny as part of our Earthly existence. Let go of too much worship of such materialism as your God, that has dominated your life right now. Let it be on a material of surviving and living just a life for God, one day at a time!

What matters at this time is that life is really simple with its simple answers and we make it more complicated as selfish Human Beings as we are blinded by the gold that we see in our eyes. If and when we truly practice our profound humility walking our lives, God will reveal the wisdom to help us become strong to practice our lives as simple and as easy as we wished it to be.

We must at this time; start the walk from our end and God will definitely meet us halfway. And when we are tired, He might even carry us on His shoulder halfway of the walk with Him. During those times of weakness, remember that God is our greatest strength! Because God loves you, He will make everything on this Earth possible for you. He can do anything with a wave of His hand, but be deserving of His gifts. That is the only thing He asked of you! God does not guarantee to walk your life for you, but He does guarantee the wisdom to bless you. God will be there to help you solve your problems in His time, but not in your expected time.

Simplify your life. Make it an easier walk. Prepare and pave the way to your true quest towards Him in his direction, and in His perfect time, that is only intended for you!

Chapter 8

The Evolving Spirit

" If I Were Your Spirit Lord"

If I were your Spirit Lord,
I will fly to the limitless skies!
I will glide in this World,
And will pass the light of Gold!
I will sprinkle your purple dust of respect, and bless this World of goodness.
No war will be amiss, because Love will be at its best!
I will evolve the highest.
I can exist the lowest!
If I were your Spirit Lord, my Spirit will rise!
But right now, I am too low to even arise!

Since the day that we are born, we are born with a soul who will evolve ultimately to be a Mature Spirit for God. With the gift of freewill that our Creator Himself has promised not to intervene out of Love, we are indeed armed and ready to face this World and this Life as a whole.

God himself has made us in his image and likeness; we are capable of the intellect of our Creator. We are armed with all the tools that are needed to deal with our whole lifetime of adventures. It is innate in each and every one of us.

The painful truth is that, we have not maximized the use of all the tools that God has already given us. We have all the tools and all of the help, but we refused to tap into it. We have been so adamant to use God's tool because we have refused to recognize Him from the very beginning of our walk. With the same ignorance, we instead turn to our pride and to our need to take full control and not surrender to God's will. Since we are not talking about a stagnated Spirit in this chapter, let's focus our attention more to the really evolving Spirit of God.

By recognizing our weaknesses through humility and by tapping into God's resources no matter what, we can continue our journey the way that God wants us to go, and the way that God also wants us to grow spiritually. In this journey, one can sometimes expect a not so comfortable sojourn.

We do not walk in this lifetime the easy way with a wide road. But our walk will be easier if we have gained the wisdom from God because our own spirit has evolved to its highest level! As I have said earlier, it is in the matter of our walk. We also do not desire God away from us in this walk. In the matter of our Spiritual maturity, we need to walk the walk in God's light and love. He is ultimately the greatest teacher that will bless us with the true wisdom that is only coming from Him.

The evolved spirit has matured and has ripened itself up for the right time. Now, it has the capability of receiving a vast pool of wisdom that is automatically given as a gift by God. We eventually profit from these vast knowledge and learning, by applying godly ways and wisdom in the practice of our lives. The soul in its lower form will now evolve slowly into full maturity; its highest level so far worthy of being God's true and Holy Spirit! The journey of an evolved spirit of God will be an easier journey. It is equipped with the tools of Eternal Alignment and wisdom. When the physical nature of a man fails, the evolved strong spirit will carry him through all the tests of his time.

The evolved spirit will then have a time on its own to adjust to such growth. The spirit of man will rise above the clouds and will communicate directly with God and he will be blessed as a favored and deserving child of God. Man will be gifted with a profound intellect of a pure spirit in the body of man! And it will be a wonderful change!

Finally, there will be no more room for ignorance and chaos. There will not be any noise to deter the man from his sublime state. There will be no more questions to ask, because the spirit has none.

The spirit and the man will be peacefully at rest. At rest from the unnecessary trivialities of life, man and spirit will be one with God's Holy Spirit! Man by then, will have more time to refocus and redirect his life to a righteous way of life! At best, confusion will now disappear in a human life, for the man and his spirit have evolved for God. What a lovely day and a lovely way to live life at last!

The adversaries of his life have disappeared like a smoke to the sky! The man has relived his life the second time around in a different light and with God's love! A total change within has just happened, where a man finally attained his well-deserved peace at last! A moment of glory and a moment of peace have just arrived on this planet.

What a wonderful moment and what a wonderful gift from God! The journey will not be a long one as long as the soul adheres to God's plans and instructions. The Spirit can ultimately expand itself to accommodate God's wisdom. And then it is ready to learn more. The higher the growth it has achieved, the more wisdom is poured to the spirit. The failures and successes of the spiritual journey are allowed for the learning process. Our pains and our sorrows are allowed to appreciate happiness along the way. This is the way of life and it is a vital part of the learning process that we have to go through.

We cannot really evolve within ourselves without the proper teachings of life itself and its surrounding circumstances in our life. It is through these experiences that we can properly attain the wisdom from what life has to offer before us.

Along the way, there will be more choices that will be made, and it will be made in God's name and in His time. **Life is the greatest teacher in our everyday living. We must not also forget that in this ailing World of ours, God is the greatest Physician that we can call at all times.**

To facilitate our healing, is for us to start our personal work helping our evolving spirit. We must look within ourselves first and then back to the World around us. We must totally accept our faults and our weaknesses and be ready to take responsibilities for our actions and not compromise the values and the virtues of life. We have to promise to change the ways that are detrimental to the growth of our spirit.

We must also provide the right healing tools to protect our ailing Spirits. When faint in the spirit, continue to feed your spirit with the prayers for strength and prayers for protection from God. He will always replenish what we need at any moment of our lives. In the past, our stagnation is of our very own doing. We have refused to listen for so long that we are almost running out of time when we have decided on our change. We have wasted so much time on the things that not important to our precious existence! And now that we are given a chance to deal with these difficulties, and now that God has given us the right tools to proceed with our life the right way, let's rejoice in God's name.

Let us embrace our inequities because by being aware of our faults, and by being humble, we can start cleaning our thoughts and our actions. We must not try to deter this wonderful spiritual growth anymore, because time is of the essence. We have to do good towards ourselves and towards one another so; we can open the door for the proper growth of our spirits.

The tests in our life, is not God's wish for damnation of His children, God only bestows the best of life for each and every one of us. But our part is to work harder to have the presence of God in our lives always! Some of the tests of our time are allowed as God's way of working His heart closer to ours.

God looks at things differently even if it may not be according to how we look at these things at our present time. Heaven's time is not the same as our time. It is totally different. God's time is always perfect. When He does answer you, exercise your patience, because He will communicate to you in His perfect time, not your expected human time!

As we try to walk with life the best that we can, our real understanding of the mysteries of how God really works in our life is not based on our understanding at the very moment, but it is based on the understanding of the wisdom that we received and gained thru Him.

The evolving Spirit can ultimately fly to its highest flight possible, and it can expand to its ultimate width to accommodate the wisdom of what it has learned from life itself with the help from God. Picture the almost perfect manifestation of a highest form of life on Earth. Mankind will be at its almost perfect growth with God's hands touching his life! His daily walk will be so blessed that he will not have a need for anything. He will be provided for everything that he need without even asking for it.

It will be a blissful existence and the return to man of his Paradise on Earth! To reestablish Paradise on Earth is not without the sacrifices involved of course! It is imperative that selfless sacrifices must be made as part of our growing spirit. Each and everyone's spirit must evolve ultimately to fulfill its destiny. We can therefore start our destiny by using the proper tools of God's Eternal Alignment.

The journey is long my dear friends, and the time is getting so close. The World has evolved faster that our very own spirit can evolve and can possibly catch up! Think deeper; maybe God is really calling you, so you won't be late, when He will arrive to claim you back in His fold. This could have been an inevitable possibility in the future of your life, and I truly believe that this could have happen to all of us at any point of time in your life and mine! The chaos of this World will eventually lead us to face our faith destiny to ultimately face God.

A faith that might be faint for most of us, but nevertheless will be the only source later on, to be the stronghold where we will stand to await our very personal judgment that will be waiting for us in the hands of God for that coming fateful day.

Our evolved Spirit by then will be ready at all times to face its anticipated future to come. May it be your heaven or mine and may it be on this World or God's, we must all be ready.

It is time and it is here and it is now. No more excuses, for such will only delay us in our preparation for a good journey. The evolved Spirits will be the only ones standing in the end. They will be the only ones that will fight for their true Master and Father in God. They will fight for the only reason, which is the reason of true love for their Heavenly Father. The only reason that spiritual strength will be recognized in its different level is not by any Human judgments, but by God's own judgment alone!

"God will continue to shower the blessings to the blessed ones. The blessed ones will be in God's favor always and nothing can harm them, as they will always be protected. They will endure the tests of their lives in flying colors, as they have lived their lives in the total surrender to God."

Love will rule their lives and endowed with the spiritual power that is only from God, they will continue to rule their life with the true wisdom from God.

My brothers and sisters let us all be reminded, that together we can be strong warriors of God to eliminate the Evil and darkness that is lurking in this World. And we can all be the blessed and the gifted ones!

Let our strength and light shine into this World where the darkness and evil are lurking and taking every opportunity to destroy us.

Let our unity for peace and love be heard across the Universe and eliminate the ultimate energy of destruction that is lurking in our immediate surroundings and future horizons!

Chapter 9

The Transformational Phase

"Behold the transformation will be near... let us prepare!
My God, my Love! I am here... I commit my life to death...
If death is love with You!
My eternal Haven in Heaven,
Please wait and wait...for thy wings are wet with the hurt...
Of hate...this Chaos from my Heart has cheated Love off and my only Spirit has left!"

"There is a phase that is inevitable in the future of this World and in our lifetime...it is the Event of the Transformation of this World."

The **Transformation** is so vast that the entire Galactic Worlds will be in total observance of this Earth when it will happen. This event, my dear brothers and sisters will be forthcoming whether we like it or not. It is to happen in this lifetime and this generation. We are overdue to receive it in God's own predicament and God's own time! This is why we are reminded to pay close attention to God's calling. This is the time to prepare us for the coming of our Heavenly Father in His full glory!

This event is the reason why you have to pay more attention to what I am going to reveal based on my visions and communication with the Heavenly Father and His Angels.

You do not have to believe me at this time, but I will reveal to you what was told to me at the time.

The event is inevitable indeed! It is getting so near, that the signs of these time, are already before your eyes and is being experienced by your heart.

The reality of these signs of time is now before your very own discernment. Feel your heart deeply, because the answer is there. Observe your surroundings, pay close attention to your natural surroundings and you will feel it so strongly.

Feel the energy of this planet, the extreme changes in the weather and nature and also see what is going on in your daily life! See your immediate surroundings and observe closely! The truth is there before your very own eyes.

This is your serious time to change, to pay close attention, and to take good care of your ailing spirit. This is the time that you must make sure to reconcile your spirit with God! This is the time to be very vigilant and be very careful in your walk with life! Each careful step that you will make will matter most for you in the future of your survival and salvation!

Why you may say now? Why did God create this wonderful World and then He takes it away from us? Well, the truth is, this is not a matter of asking God Why He is doing what He is doing to us now, so we can blame him because of our ignorance. This is not the time to be ignorant! This is the time that you will need to work harder to receive the wisdom from God to help you endure the tests of time and to help you to answer all your questions in life!

It is not the how, the why and the when. This is an event that has to take place, to purify this World from the filth that we have wallowed in such a long time! We have allowed the Devil to stay here and fathered this World for too long. Since we have turned our backs away from God for too long, it is responsibility now to give Him back the respect and the love that He truly deserves! We cannot continue living this façade that you call, **"your way of life."** Our life has to change for the better at the least, with God in it. The excuses that we have made in the past, will not work anymore for the present time, and in our future life. If we want to survive these tests of life, we must strengthen our spirits and mature it to be able to receive God's blessings and wisdom for our ultimate survival! Survival tools will be needed at that time.

There is no taking it easy anymore. We have to take this event seriously, because we have wasted enough time already. We may have to act a little quicker now before it is too late! This is the time for man's moment of truth. And this is the time that we have to pay heed and not ignore the messages! Perhaps we can start by organizing our life based on our priorities. This is the time to prioritize the inclusion of growing our spirit for God. When the time comes that everything else will fail, it is only a strong spirit that will be able to endure and survive in the end to be with God! Our disobedience and the wrong priorities in the way we have lived our lives, have placed as back and as far away from God as possible. We have long forgotten the real essence of our creation and real purpose on this planet.

We need to work harder to get ourselves back in God's good hands. He is the only Savior and Protector that we will need in the end! Lastly we also forgot that this is a temporary World, created by our very own Creator and Heavenly Father in Heaven.

When the time will come when He will reclaim us back to His fold, we will not have any say about it! It is totally up to Him when and how He will do it! If Earth is pregnant, it is nine months pregnant and is long overdue to deliver its unfolding inevitable transformation! You may not understand me at this time, but I can assure you that if you could have been a grown Spirit right now, you will understand me without any question.

My dear brothers and sisters in God, please observe the changes in the World around you. Isn't it obvious enough for you to see? Feel it in your heart and spirit and try to discern. What about the alarming changes with Mother Earth itself!

The extreme changes of weather and nature are very obvious to the entire World. Signs abound everywhere and are reflecting an evident impending catastrophic signs of our time. I will not predict the exact time or place because I am not God. But what I can tell you is that when God's messenger, St Michael, will tell you that **"we are running out of time and it is now that we pay heed to God!"** What would that mean for you and me? What is God's time and what is really your time? It is all up to you. I am just relaying to you the messages that I was told, when God touched me! I was not ready to even imagine the look of concern that I have seen from the face of an Archangel!

And perhaps, you can never imagine me, face to face with that particular encounter! And face to face with St. Michael, a very high ranking of all Archangels? One thing that I can tell you though, that particular encounter, came to me with such disbelief at first, (perhaps a normal reaction from an imperfect human being like me of course!) but then; it has opened my eyes for the truth of how seriously the Angel meant it! And it dawned on me how helpless I could have felt in my heart, when this time will really come to the future of my life and yours.

The Angel, St. Michael then showed me a glimpse of that future certainty! And before I can even react, I was already balling my eyes out because the pain that I have felt was so overwhelming and the visions that I saw was too terrifying for me!

I will keep this encounter and visions in my heart forever, for in my heart, at this present time, I would just like to focus on making a difference in your life and mine, with all the positive inspiration that is humanly possible on this planet. We will need it to make our spirit strong together!

I will only try to focus on what will help us in the future according to God's teachings. I have learned a very overwhelming crash course from the Heavenly Masters themselves, and I will only relay the message based on how I was taught, nothing added, and nothing removed. I will refuse to make intentional mistake by them. To be a responsible person is to make the right judgment call at anytime of you're day and night with no excuses. This is a very private and personal experience for me that you may not believe. My only wish for you is just to have an open mind and if unsure, turn to God for your answers and please discern and make sure that you are not praying to the wrong God.

Remember that the true God is in Heaven and He is truly an embodiment of true love. And the lessons that He will wish you to learn are about lessons of love and light. If there is even a glimmer of darkness involved, it is not coming from the God in Heaven! There are two (2) co-existences that play a vital role to the lives of all Human Beings on this planet. As the God of love and of light have all His Heavenly Angels and influences over men, so does the prince of darkness who will also have his dark angels to fool you. So be careful, be wary and if you are disturbed and feeling lost and unprotected, call for God's Angels in Heaven to guide and protect you always!

The right answers for your lessons in life will be attained soon. When you are ready, God will provide you with all the answers! The wisdom that you will be given will be a tremendous amount of knowledge that will help you in your entire life!

In the future, when you learn the right ways of God, you will be able to get your life back and be in control of all your actions and responsibilities. In God's hands, you will be also safe and protected! Believe in yourself and have faith with Him. He will be there always to guide and protect you. Remember how special you are to God and keep that knowledge in your heart! When you believe, do not question the wisdom of God's teachings. Only question those things that do not pertain to love and to the spreading of good light. Discern all messages and communication properly thru the work of the Holy Spirit.

Above all stay away from darkness! Please do not doubt this Galactic event! Do not even try to entertain the doubts to cloud your mind and Spirit; you will experience the truth while reading this book. God has already provided you with the wisdom to understand me without any resistance. So start now and open your hearts and mind to the lessons of love.

I just wanted to get your attention at this point, initially we will not be able to agree to disagree, because the truth of the matter is, I was given the privilege to have a little peek of the future of this World, and I have been revealed the signs that is already happening at this present time. Personally, the experience between God and I, took me years and a lot of tears, holy water and prayers, to properly comprehend the depth of such mystical experience and it was beyond any of my human control. In all my life, I would never in my conscious life just accept the anything that I cannot control. But believe me when I tell you, that with God, you will not have any control. Ready or not, when He touches you, you will have to will Him your will if He wants it. He will teach you how to properly discern with the Discernment of the Holy Ghost.

And He will guide you the way, but the walk later on will be the hardest because the truth and the awareness are sometimes too painful to carry. Like you before, I was very stubborn and skeptical about what had happened to me, when God touched me.

I was not ready for Him and I was questioning my worth and my lowly life in comparison to the attention that He has given me in that particular time of my life. And I was not ready for Him. But He was there and in His full glory, revealed the future of this World and the grief of His heart. I have felt so much love that I have never felt before in His presence.

"**The hand of my Father in Heaven is about to touch the Universe. My Father is in too much grief because His people are turning their backs away from Him and He is in pain.**"

After Jesus said this, I saw from the corner of my eye, a vision of a very huge hand that is almost about to touch a vision of a rounded globe with the map of the whole world. The globe is so small compared to the huge hand, it almost looked like a little speck of dust on a very huge hand. If that was God's hands, Earth is almost like just a speck of dust in His Hands! Very tiny speck of dust indeed! And at that time, I wondered if we are worth the attention that God has given us.

As if to answer my question, God has shown me how He has loved us so much, that He even sent His only Begotten Son to rescue and redeem us from all of our sins! What an awe-inspiring message for all of us! And I am happy to give you that news!

You might be thinking at this time to beware of false prophets. And I totally agree with you. I can assure you that I will never claim myself as a prophet of some kind. I will even refuse to call me nothing other than just a humble servant who has decided now to walk with God.

I am only relaying to you the messages that I was told to share to help God's other children, believers or non-believers to give them a chance with God and His kingdom. You have a choice to believe or not to believe me, because it is a matter of a question of faith in your life. I will only narrate to you my personal spiritual encounter with the Holy Family and God's Angels and Spiritual messengers. I will not force you to believe me or to continue to read this book if you are not ready at this time.

Whether you will believe me or not, I will totally refuse to add or delete the gist of this spiritual encounter, because I will surely displease God and I am surely not going to disappoint Him because of your own disbelief and caring what you have to say! It is not your experience, but mine. In a way, I was adamant to accept the gifts that were given to me, because I had a very confused Spirit just like anybody else in this planet at that time.

To experience an amazingly mystical and profound spiritual encounter was pretty overwhelming. That's not even including the profound revelation about life, and the future peek of this World. Here, I have given you a peek of my personal experience, so you will understand where I am coming from. I just hope that you will continue to open your mind and always pray for your answers from God if you are unsure of your answers!

There was a tremendous amount of responsibility that was expected of me at that time. When you are mature in the Spirit, you will know that God's gifts are not really gifts, but they are really a tremendous amount of responsibility that is expected of you to be able to maintain such gifts. I just wanted you to know that to understand this part of the few revelations, will help you to work harder on yourself and your Spirit to grow right.

The other purpose is saving your spirit from your ultimate destruction because you have not followed God's orders in your life. If there is a chance to grow your Spirit and to change at this time, be conscious now of all your actions. Avoid the path of destruction that you have done in the past. God is now giving you a chance to redeem yourself thru this book! Prioritize your life and start working with God as your first priority. If you are walking the wrong path, change your direction and redirect your focus to keep the healthy relationship between you and God!

Do not even open the door that will compromise your Spiritual health! Proceed with caution if faced with a situation to accomplish the wrong priorities that will lead to your own inevitable Spiritual demise, and turn away from the bad influences in life! The transformation in itself will be the judging stage of life as played by you.

There will be numerous players; the actors and actresses of life itself cannot escape the final judgment and one of them will be you! Each and every role of a Human life will be played in detail before God in His Kingdom and before the final curtains will fall. We will all be judged according to the merits that we have built in our names, and according to the merits that we have done to God's other children on Earth!

The Transformation is a very serious event for all of mankind. This is where you have to choose your side whether you are ready or not. This is the event that is the only chance in your life, and for your Spirit, to live forever with the Eternal Father as a grand price. This is the chance that will finalize your borrowed life and will determine the quality of your Spiritual walk. It is very important for me to reveal this part of my experience with God, because this is an imperative knowledge that you must keep forever in your Heart. Be aware that this is the generation that God has already planned to visit in the future!

We will eventually experience this Transformation that will happen in this lifetime, and in this generation. This is a profound experience that will make you witness God's Eternal Power in action and in His full glory. Here, you will also be a witness of the battle between good and evil before your very eyes. In the end, you will be forced to choose sides and depending on how you have played your role in this lifetime, you will know which side you will be in.

As I have stated in the previous pages of this book. Pay attention and slowly acquire the knowledge and the wisdom to prepare for this time. I wanted you to have a little peek of what was revealed to me to give you the privilege of knowing what you cannot achieve at this time. Put your priorities in order and prepare yourself for that walk with God and for your own revelation in your future and final walk of life!

While learning to walk the walk, there is also an expectation that you should place upon yourself to grow your Spirit in the maturity and readiness to be able to face God Himself in your judgment time, and in the preparation for this event that is inevitably apparent and is inevitable in your future. I can only humble myself to share the truth that will be kept in my heart forever for it is this particular truth that has given me so much fear for those Spirits who are not ready for God in the future.

The reality of this event as I have remembered, would be a reality that is an overwhelming impending transformation that could and will happen as part of the future of this World. This transformation is still too vivid in my visions that just to think about it makes my heart stopped for a moment!

The reality of this Galactic event is so humongous that I do not think I want to wish this certain future event upon my future life, nor to the future of the ones that I love.

To the rest of the people on this World, I am hoping that you will open up your mind now to the truth that was revealed for you in this book! At this point, although God has given us the tools to prepare ourselves, we still. have to do our work. I would also like to take this opportunity to say to you for the millionth times, to be open to learn and embrace all the positive changes in your lives and your spirits so we can still be called the least of God's children! As God has loved us for all eternity and so should we give love back that He truly deserves.

Ready or not we will ultimately go back to our Creator in the final judgment of our time. May it be your lifetime or your children's lifetime, be ready at all times.

Look forward to the future and make your daily lives the best days of your life! Put righteousness in front of you and do not waver in your faith with God. Put honesty and love as part of your dealings with others and avoid the darkness that will try to stop you in your humble walk for God! This is the time to obey God's commandments. This is a chance to regain back God's blessings and trust, and a time of growing one's Spirituality.

The present moment where you can be reborn again to honor yourself like you never did before, while attaining the peace that you have been missing your entire life.

As we continue this sojourn, we will be in the midst of a transformation of the events in our lives. We will be more aware to the ways of the World, because we are now more careful in the walk that we will later on undertake. Now we can place more value in what matters most in our lives.

Every minute and every hour that will pass us through, we will always breathe a new life of love around us and we shall live every moment like it is our last!

In the future of this World...The Vision as revealed!
The First Vision

It is a certain time, where the weather will suddenly change. The temperature will suddenly drop so cold. Then as if the time itself will stop! It will be so quiet and so odd...then something else happens...

There is a time of discord and chaos on Earth. Satan is awake! His demons will be walking on this Planet. Below, there will be some sort of volcanic eruption in the ground. The Earth's crust will open up and then I saw creatures, monsters and demons, spiritual shadows appearing everywhere.

The dead will start to appear from the core of the Earth, and they all will walk the lands of this planet! Then, darkness will cover this Planet. And the sun itself will somehow disappear from sight! What a sudden change for the whole World!

Then the whole World will suddenly become very quiet and very eerie...Suddenly, I heard this voice saying, **"Look up...The Almighty God of All, is coming in His Full Glory!"** Then I heard thunder and lightning race the sky! Up in the sky, I saw a vision of the millions of light, lighting the whole sky! I saw white horses coming down from God's Heaven and each one of the horses has a rider. As the horse became clearer to my view, I saw that the rider is an Angel wearing a white robe and holding the horse with his left hand, I noticed that he is waving a big silver sword in his right hand. And then, on his left side like a partner in war, I also noticed the Angel's companion.

This man is wearing a dark brown robe with a sash of brown rope tied around his waist. He was gliding like in a time suspension, his speed is in accordance with the speed of the white horse and its rider and they come down like this in pairs of twos by the thousands, maybe by the millions as if ready for war. Earth will be burning with all kinds of fire everywhere and then, Earth start to vigorously shake nonstop for three to 8 days. Rain starts to fall all over the World. But wait a minute! It is not rain of water but a heavy rain of fire!

In Heaven, the three Angels are about to blow their individual Horns and Trumpets. They were floating in front of Heaven's Church, the one Angel in the center is robed in white and is suspended a little bit higher that the two Angels on each of her side. The two Angels on the side are also robed in white and each one held a Trumpet that they are about to blow.

Inside Heaven's Church, Angels of different orders are singing words of praise to God sitting up on what sort to look like an Altar and the Sun behind Him looking down upon what seemed to be a Royal Throne."

" A Centerpiece of Worship!"

I exclaimed silently and joyously, for there is nothing on this Earth that can be compared to the overwhelming sight inside this magical and celestial Church Palace of God the Father! Angels in a Choir surrounded the Throne centered on the middle of this Church. And then God gave a silent command and everybody obeyed without questions or resistance! I was also surprised to see that my spirit was in the same level of obedience at that time. Then an Angel said to me, "You have just witness the display of "Oneness with God!"

Everywhere, all kinds and types of Angels and Celestial beings, even royalty representatives of God's kingdom, in beautiful gowns and robes and scepters and crowns! What an amazing sight to behold! Beauty and the display of love emanating from their spiritual bodies! Joyful songs were sung of praise and honor for God, sitting on His throne with a crown of the Holy Trinity on His head! He was wearing a pure white robe and holding what seemed to be a wooden staff!

God was sitting in front of the Sun! The sunrays are coming through Him from the back! The Sun light though was not blinding, was giving Him a display of pure power of energy! Music continually engulfed the entire Church with songs of such beautiful melodies!

The Angels are beautifully robed Ethereal Beings that are exuding love from just their mere Spiritual display of Humanness and just by their main presence. I heard the songs…Angels are singing Glory be… Gloria and Hallelujah…Our father etc. continually to the Heavenly Father in his Throne." Tirelessly they sang in total magnificent display of goodwill and loyalty to God!

The Second Vision as Revealed!

The Other Visions of Spiritual Warfare as revealed…then on a different dimension of space and time that I cannot tell, I saw a huge Dragon! His face is like half human and half monster's face.

Very menacing look in his eyes. A look of hatred and despise against God! He has a big horn protruding from the center of his forehead! He is covered all around with the scales of a Dragon!

He was kicking and angry when I see him in this vision. This half Dragon, half Man, was trying to hit me with his tail that looked like a big long tail with a sharp spear at the end of it.

Then I saw myself holding a big silver sword in my right hand opposite to this half Man, half Dragon.

In this particular vision, I have also transformed into a spiritual being, ready to fight this Dragon side by side with the presence of the Holy Family and all of God's Angels!

"I would like to pause at this particular point of writing this chapter, because I want to offer my personal prayer with you for the Heavenly Father."

My Offertory Prayer

"My Father in Heaven, through the examples of Jesus Christ, your only Begotten Son, whom you have sent to this planet to redeem all of us from our sins that He did not commit, and because of His profound love for us, He gave His life, to give all of us a chance for a new beginning. To all the Angels and Saints of God, that have helped and protected us, I thank you for giving me the opportunity to cleanse my Spirit from the stain that I have carried for a long time through this book. On my bended knees, I humbly ask forgiveness for my sins and I offer all the happiness that I have experienced on Earth because of your blessings Lord. For all that I am, and for all that I will become, I surrender to your will Father. I put my life on your hands and in my final moment, please receive me in your Kingdom, Father in Heaven. Amen."

The Transformational Phase is near and it is coming! I feel it in my heart and I am pretty sure you are feeling it too. The signs of times are before us. The energy of change is pretty strong. Our World's energy is getting heavier to carry.

Time and weather has changed so much as revealed to me in the year 1998. I am seeing that the future transformation is inevitable and I felt it so much that it is soon. My concern is not the event itself, but my personal concern is if each and every one of us will be ready to face our true Father in the future, and if we are ready to shape His ideal "Paradise in Earth". I know the hesitation that you might perhaps feel whether to believe what I am saying here. But I can assure you that the truth lies deep in your very Heart and Soul. You have felt the signs and have seen the events of your life. Do not be blinded by the lies and the liars that abound on this Planet! The truth sometimes although painful can be a freeing reality if you just embrace it. Each one has the capability of discernment and intelligence.

We are born with this innate and is a God given gifts that sometimes we refuse to use because we have the need to take control and we have a hard time to surrender to anything or to anybody other than ourselves. Pride and ego have always played a major role in our decision-making and thus helped in the stagnation of our Spiritual growth. Let go of your control. Put your life in a safe place or in God's hands! Please do not try to analyze too hard what I am trying to say to you here. Let your thoughts flow without resistance and only feel how your heart felt after you read this book.

Have God's automatic wisdom and Holy Spirit flow through you without resistance. As life is your teacher, God is your best Professor. He is your only teacher here in this Book. I am just trying to communicate to you how I can help you open the door to your soul and to join me in my journey to help you in your quest for God and then have Him work on you.

God will communicate to you in the language that you can understand and in the level of your Spiritual growth. Hold on to your Spirit and soar! Accommodate the wisdom that is there ready for you to receive. Expand you spirit as deep and wide as you can handle. The gifts from God are automatic to be given to you when you are ready. Be open and do not resist Him anymore. It is time and it is right now! Be serious about the things and events that will inevitably affect your life in the future. Do not play games anymore. Be assured of a protected life in God. Goodness is never enough as well as your kind acts of goodness. To obey God's teaching is a must at this time!

The Transformational Phase is real and it is evidently shown in the events that are happening in our lives. It will happen to this World! If you do not believe, please do not mock the truth. The truth is only the beginning of our journeys, and the rest will be up to us! So go and spread the word of God to your brethren and always make the right choices in your lives and be one with God's Spirit and blessings. When you practice your life, give Love to the rest of your brethren, there is never enough Love given to this World!

Chapter 10

The Miracles Received

"You Are The Miracle Of Creation"

You have dearly touched my Heart!
My Love Eternal...I breathe life into you ...and my Spirit follow!
Be deserving of my love, be the miracle of my light!
I have exhausted the sky and send my cries...in search of You, because you said goodbye!
My Miracle!
My Creation!
Where are you?
I love you!
Remember I alone, have created You!

Alas! The vessel of God! Many will be called, but so very few will be chosen! When God will seek you out, be ready for what is to become of you! You will learn to exercise your faith like you never did before and learn to humble your life according to God's will. Whether you are ready or not, it will not matter anymore, because He will touch your life anyway, just because you deserved it at that time! You may ask yourself why would God do something unexpected like this to happen to anyone? Well the answer to your question will be because; God works in His own time not yours.

If God will decide to touch a very bad sinner, at a certain point of somebody's life that you really knew, who does not even deserve God's presence, God has always have a reason for doing so. God has a unique plan for each one of His individual creations. We have no right, in any circumstance of our life, to point a finger and judge any other fellow human being or judge any of God's actions. It is not up to us to judge anything living or non-living things, because it all up to the Creator of all of us...who is God, to ultimately make the judgment in the end!

So in this lifetime, the miracles of life from God can only be received in the form of Spiritual gifts and wisdom. Whoever will receive such gifts will be called the blessed children of God.

Though physically they are still living, a gifted person will know another gifted one, through the process of their own mature Spiritual discernment. They do not have to necessarily communicate to each other physically, but they can receive and feel each other through their own ways of communication of their minds and their Spirits! Eventually, they will continue to evolve with the wisdom of the truth of God's ways. They are the growing visionaries of this World. When you observe a growing number of true visionaries all over this World, do not be alarmed! This is the definite sign of the time.

This is very evident right now at this present time, because there will be end times messengers, that have been already touched by God with different missions to carry, to pave the way for the coming of the big transformation that will happen in the future of this World!

God has already sent His very own Spiritual Angels and Spiritual Warriors on this planet to protect you in the future of what is to happen! They are already here and are walking with you and experiencing the same pain and frustration that God's Heart is experiencing, because of our own wrong doings, pride, and disobedience. **The gifted Human Beings are a pure and simple example of a group of people living on this planet that have already matured in their Spirit and attained some degree of holiness in God's eyes, because of the good deeds that they have done for the other children of God.**

They have not ascended yet, because they have to stay a while, to fulfill their individual gifts of helping God to return us back to Him. Also, to increase the awareness of the masses of this World to pay attention to God's words now, before the end of our time! These are the special few children of God in their individual gifts. They apply their special gifts and talents according only to God's instructions, and they have already surrendered their own life and freewill to be used by God! They are all humble servants in total surrender of their whole life for God.

They are the miracles that already happened to this planet. You can tell them by the way they have walked their lives. They are mostly in pain than the ordinary people that did not grow their Spirits yet, because they are constantly aware of the pain of God's Heart and the sufferings of their own people in this World.

The ascended gifted Spirits are more powerful in Heaven than the living ones on Earth. They are called the honored Saints of Heaven! They could either be male or female holy Spirits that have ascended. They have all physically died on Earth! Since they are now in pure Spirits, they have the "**power of intercession.**"

The people on Earth when they have the need for somebody to intercede for them during their difficult times, they can call on these purified Saints for help. They are stationed to listen for anybody that will need them at any moment in time! Believe that there are such an existence of an elevated living and non-living Human Beings!

The Saints do exist in this World and in Heaven. These are the rewarded and the already favored children of God.

God and His Angels are continually watching and are continually protecting these gifted ones, because they have already passed their Spiritual tests in their lifetime! Do not mock these special people of God! You will answer personally to God when you do! That is why I have to make my points clear to you that be careful not to judge anyone harshly, because you do not know who is behind them!

I cannot emphasize well enough to be very careful with each step that you take in this World! Your actions could be very harmful to your growing spirits.

Ask God for help and do not succumb to negativism and despair! Make the wisdom that you have learned and practiced, be the start of your inspiration to your infinite happiness! On the other hand, do not get fooled by false prophets and fake visionaries. The Prince of the Dark World, who totally hated Human Beings, and totally abhors God's love and kindness to us, will also send his Demonic Angels and so called visionaries!

Discern and differentiate the Angels of light from God, from the demonic Angels of the darkness from the other side. They are all very powerful than you can ever imagine. Side with God and be careful that you do not fall into the pit of darkness, which will trap and trash your spirit to destruction away from God! The choice is not by God's alone!

The answer is inside your heart and in your growing Spirit. Fight back evil to regain control of your life again and your loved ones. Stay away from the dark corners of your life. Stay strong in the arms of your Savior, in the arms of your mighty Father in Heaven!

You have the choice! It is up to you to receive your very unique gifts that have been waiting there for you to use. You are God's most special miracle that He had created out of pure Love! He has already given you the innate inner light inside of you through your spirit to guide you. When your life journey began a long time ago, God and his messengers have been also working hard by you, with you and around you.

You have been surrounded by the power of protection and love by your Almighty Father Himself! Haven't you noticed? Have you been ungrateful? I hope not. For your own sake, go back and renew your life to the fullest! Be grateful for the blessings that you have received from your Heavenly Father above! Pay attention and understand the real reason and the real meaning of your life! Understand your purpose in life. Be the vessel that is created by pure Love from the very beginning of time. Remember now that the miracles and the gifts from God, does not always come in big packages. God's powerful gifts sometimes come in humble little packages! One miracle already happened in your life, and you are one of them! Be thankful for all the blessings small or big that happened to you. Ask yourself a question and be honest now.

How many times in your life, that even for a brief moment in your everyday journey with life, that you have paused for a few minutes, to give thanks to this wonderful Universe and to your Creator and Protector for all your blessings?

Have you been too busy to even pay a little attention to those little minute details that are important to your life and to the growth of your spirit? What are your important priorities? Miracles cannot be received if we refuse to make a very important change in our lives. We have been lost too long and although we always wanted control, we are actually out of control in our lives. An unfortunate mishap that can easily be corrected, if we can accept to humble ourselves and change our lives for the better and start a new life with God again!

If you believe, it is time to use the Eternal Tools Of Alignment With God. This is your chance for Spiritual redemption. It is here and ready for you to grasp it! Learn and use it for your own good and teach others. You are indeed God's miracle. Prove it to Him now because this time is the right time and He is now calling you back.

Open up your lives to be led to the best destination that is only Heaven. We must not resist the innate wisdom that has always been there to be tapped into. We have the most powerful resources that do not cost us a single dime, but will cost us a great deal of sorrow and pain, if we must misuse it. Clean up not only your body, but also your mind of filth; hatred, prejudices and pride. Start with a humble, clean and sanctified body!

Be ready to receive God's Holy Spirit to guide you in the right direction of your lives. Now is the time not just to receive His gifts and be called the "Gifted One", but also use such valuable gifts, to help others to receive their gifts as well.

Let it begin with you, and let yourself spread all the Love that you can give. Help others to grow their Spirits, and also help them achieve the ultimate happiness from their own Spiritual quest!

Receive the miracles of God and live in peace with yourself and with others in total harmony and oneness with God's Spirit. Attain you most deserving, "Oneness with God" that is now your special relationship with your Creator and Heavenly Father. You have become one with Him and Him in you. Believe that you are now being protected, guided, and loved for all of Eternity!

This time you will realize that destiny is now indeed anticipated with joyfulness in your heart! So look forward to the love and lights that only God can provide! It is indeed a very wonderful experience to be at peace with oneself and be at peace with the environment. This is peace that cannot be disturbed just so easily. This is a state of some wonderful feeling, that is only exclusive, and intimately yours to treasure and enjoy.

Your gifts will become you. You have become strong for God in your walk, because you have used His Eternal Tools to help and guide you. You have not doubted Him when you used His tools, because you knew deep in your Heart that it will work in the end! Beyond all possible reasonable doubts, you have followed His beautiful and positive teachings of love and lights, to surround your every journey!

Alas! You have become the rarest gem in the rough! The ocean of obstacles will try to spread its water of fear to your growth but you now know better, because you have become invincible to destroy!

You have now fought for your Father as a true warrior with the strength of Hercules! With the same blind obedience, you will keep going no matter what, because you now know the clear way of the right path to follow.

You will become Spiritually mature and aware that through your partnership with God and His guidance, you are ready to discern with the wisdom that God has given you for being an obedient child! And you are now ready to face God's truth! From now on, you will proceed with caution in dealing with your life. You will make a big difference in changing other people's lives for the better! You will take to your heart, that you are just a humble servant for God.

You will always be firmly grounded, for you will become the epitome of Humility for all to see. Other people will probably see you weak, but it does not matter, because you knew that your humility is God's greatest strength.

You will ultimately receive the miracles from God through your very own efforts of making a difference to other people's lives other than your own. Your goal will be to replicate yourself in not just by making money, but saving a soul, one soul at a time in God's name.

These are just but a few of the ways to get God's attention, by helping His other children in need. Remember, regardless of who you are; we are all equal in God's eyes. Any display of pride from your side will disconnect you to the righteous ways that are not of God's.

Any negative display whether from an emotional side, physical, mental or spiritual could affect your connection with God. If you do happen to fail somewhat in your walk, ask forgiveness and repent. Do not stain yourself again by failing to stand corrected the second time around. Do not burn your bridges with God. Keep it intact for it will be your ultimate way to return to Him in the end of your life journey.

Live the miracles today. With a changing World and tough economic times, the only power you will need is to be strong by God and leave the rest to Him. Accept the things that you cannot change and change the things for the better. Let God be your leader in every direction and choices that you will make.

Life is easier when you understand the full meaning of surrender. A tough Spirit will endure the tests of time. These are trying times when reality itself presents a real danger to the staining of the Spirit of man, and when misdirection and rationalization becomes the normal way of life for an ailing Spirit and this ailing World. For now, we have to keep away from misdirected thoughts, and bad judgments leading to our poor actions. We have to be wary of too much temptation that is worst for our inner Spiritual health. And let us focus on creating and nurturing the health of our fellow brethren in God.

Any Human Being with a good Spiritual health walks hand in hand with God. Keep your healthy relationship with God! He will always be there to pick up the pieces of your life. Although, like everyone else, any man will be bombarded with obstacles of his daily life, but a strong man with God in his life, will always come out victorious in whatever decision that he will undertake, because he will rule his life with the wisdom from God.

Anything else that he cannot handle he let God handle it for Him. The miracle of Human existence is in the health of the Human Spirit. The mature and healthy Spirit, will have all the wisdom it will need to rule his life, and become the miracle himself. Meanwhile, he will continue to help more spiritual vessels to experience their own individual miracles of life too!

A peaceful existence, and an abundance of the miracles of Love on this Planet, is like experiencing Heaven on Earth at these temporal times. When a possible future, and when men will change for God, Paradise on Earth will be reestablished again! This will be a World of peace and love. A World of ascended Human Beings in their pure Spirits.

Meanwhile, here are my cheers to your Spirit! You are now near God's heart! You are so close to Him now. Be patient, you are almost there! As He showers you with wisdom and love, rejoice in His name for you are now a favored Child of God!

"Believe in the forgiveness of Love, as Sorrow will drown the Pain. Give delight to the Heart that is abandoned in Christ!"

Chapter 11

The Heart of Gold

"Not Of This Earth!"

This little man,
This big Spirit,
Amazing speed of Light!
This color of the Day,
This journey of faith,
This growing in Life!
As I ponder the moments,
The moments of Love!
Engulfed with Gold,
Strength of Hercules,
Light of Zeus,
With thunder, return to Gold!
Heart of Silver Dewy Nights,
Tears of Joy,
Man of God,
Not of this Earth!

Once the living Spirit of man has evolved and received the true miracles of merits from God, The growing individual Spirit will be in a transformed Human Being. The highest form that God has created with Love! As if born anew with the new zest for life, the renewed Sprit will totally turn around to start a new journey with God. He will be full of gifts and blessings.

He will be endowed with the wisdom and the Spiritual strength of the whole army of God! He will lead the way to the life of enlightenment. Only God knows the limits of his power, because he will walk with Him always!

Armed with the Heart of Gold, he is ready to face life, and battle its obstacles with more ammunition of peace and love than he can muster. The way that he will view life, will also change and this time, for the better! He will see his World in a different light! He will light the dark corners of this Planet emanating from his own light and his mere presence. He will carry the light of God, and some torches of life for God's other children.

He will become the strong anchor of the faint of hearts. He will be an exemplary example of the true display of compassion of the heart, because this man will cry the tears of other people's pain! The beauty of this special man will now exude from within, as his Spirit will glow to the tempo of his miraculous life! There is no superficiality in his action, for he is determined to stand by the virtues that he stood for in God's name.

His lifetime will be full of adventures and wisdom gained! With so much gusto, he will perform more efficiently than just a regular man, for he possesses none of that self serving pride but, more of a universal understanding of the meaning of his true existence; that he only offers for God. He will also become aware that this time, he could control his walk in the right path, and with the wisdom of the truth that is only coming from God! His self-serving days are over, and he will now begin to do everything with so much love in his eyes.

He becomes the Universal Man of God. He is a man of the World with a Heart of Gold! A Human Being almost perfect for the World and serving only God! He will be judged by the selflessness of his actions and his peers will love him. He is a very respectable man in every aspect of his life. He will continue to grow indeed, and will be a pleasing sight in God's eye. Beyond all his wealth of wisdom and servitude, he will balance his life with a giving heart, a heart of gold! In the future, he may well be adorned with all the material things of life, but his heart of gold will prevail in all of his life! This man will lead a life of compassion and will inspire hope in every direction that will pass his life.

What an amazing journey, and what an amazing man! This man will keep lasting friendships along the way, and loving relationships that are built by compassion and love. He will inspire hope to those that are lowly, and will intimidate those who are proud, because he knew better to stay away from pride!

As he treads through his own life journey, he will continue to grow in accordance with God's values and virtues! And he will leave a trail of good deeds, as examples for mankind to follow! He is an evolved Spirit in action. He will lead by example, he will not rule by his brawn. His faith for God is unwavering, and his good-natured ways will be innumerable. He will help to spread the gifts of the Spirit. He will continue to spread the light in this World. The light of God will start to shine from within him, because he will glow in the darkest point of somebody's life! He may as well live in a castle made of gold, but humility will continue to guide his ways amidst the material riches of his world.

He will lead other people to the right directions of their lives! He will be anchored firmly and strongly on the ground and in perfect condition. Obstacles and tests will not easily weaken him like an ordinary man, because he is not the ordinary man anymore.

The man that I am talking about is almost not of this World! But he is in this World! It is our chance to grow like him right now. This is a possibility that could happen to you in your future life on this planet! This is such a reality that I am wishing for all of us to follow. As I am writing this book, I am also learning with you. I am writing all these messages that can only be inspired by the lights and love of God for all of us! These are messages that are only inspired by His loving ways!

A man with a heart of gold is a wishful possibility. But we can make this a probable reality if we can at least try to grow our Spirits in the right direction. God has been patiently waiting for us to come back to him, and He would not mind to wait a little bit more if we should at least try.

It will be a hard life for those who cannot fathom the depth of his existence, but nonetheless, he will be most praised in all of his actions. A man with the Heart of Gold will unite one another, to the ultimate journey for peace, and no war will happen if we can recreate ourselves to be like him! Armed with the Heart of Gold, this compassionate example of a merciful and an almost perfect man, will pave the way for the peace that was once unattainable. If all men will be transformed like him, love will reign in any region of chaos, and peace will abundantly flow on this Planet! The strong character and personality that will be exuded from this man is extraordinary but wonderful! Like a stronghold of a human being, robust enough to make a very intimidating and wonderful impression!

There will be no point to doubt his honesty, because he only tells the truth. He will not hesitate to decline the invitations to join the façade of the most immature spirits by refusing to lace his words with the lies from the darkness. He will be straight in his answers and will be short in his responses. He believed very deeply in conserving his energy to serve only one master, and that is…His Heavenly Father! Not of this World!

I said to myself. I was a little confused, when I picture this man that I can imagine to be of a rare breed. And then, I had a very strong realization! We have already had this man on this planet and that is our very own Savior, and best example to follow… Jesus Christ! Just imagine the walk of this man.

Isn't everything that I have described is a perfect description of Jesus Christ's loving and humble but strong ways? There was a time, when the only Begotten Son of God was sent to show us the way? And was Jesus ways the core examples of true love, sacrifice and humility for all to follow? Didn't He show us also His heart of gold? Didn't he say before that He is the Way to His Father? Jesus did show true love for us on this World, but in return, we have shown Him our real gratitude, by sacrificing Him to die on the Cross! Like before, we have fallen prey to our pride, prejudices and ignorance! We have been so stubborn to pay attention to the subtlety of the messages that was for us to discern and follow. We have lost the chance before, and I am wishing that this book would open the door to our second chance again, to learn and practice His ways, back in our lives!

As Jesus Christ died for us, to redeem us from the sins that He did not commit, here we are still acting so spoiled and very ungrateful! At the present times, we have shown our ingratitude by continuing to ignore the meaning of Jesus death for us on the cross. We have not been so sorry in our ways. As a matter of fact, we are ignoring the walk that Jesus has always wanted us to take for our own good. Nothing has changed for us then, and nothing will change for us now. It has always been our option to use our freewill to make the righteous moves, but we have refused all these for nothing. In the end, we have compromised our very soul to despair and confusion.

The confusion that will ultimately lead us to our own spiritual destruction! At the present time, we have ignored the lessons that we could have learned from our past mistakes. We have denied ourselves the tools that could have helped to make us strong in life! We have continued to displease ourselves, and we have continued to move forward towards the journey to the lost land. Onward we go to the very empty land to the point of no return! Maybe the end will lead us to a new beginning of life.

The choice is yours to take and all other options are open at the present time as well. Meanwhile the man with a heart of gold will continue to haunt our dark shadows. He will continue in his loving ways to help you. You will be the most work in His whole life. But he would not mind. For him, your spiritual growth will be as important to him than his own.

His work will not be done until he successfully save one soul at a time, and put them back to God where they belong. He has already attained the level of a spiritual growth to the point that he knows your growing pains.

He wanted to make sure that you too could share the same peace and the same strength that he has attained in his life! As he goes, he will not mind your stubborn ways, because he just care for you to change in your own pace, and in your own good time! In the future, he will wish you to be in the oneness in the spirit with God. He will guide and help you even till the end of his life, to prove to you the beauty of the love that is only coming from God! This Human Being is you and I my dear friends. We are equally given the chance to mature and to grow our Spirits, in unison with God's own spirit.

This is the highest possible goal that you should achieve in this lifetime, and in this planet! Let us all transform in goodness and in unity, let us all hold hands and join this man! We can only join him if we can start our change now. It is not too late. Although time is a changing, we are still given the moments of our life to change. This change is needed in the future, but this is the time to start the journey! We have exhausted our excuses.

There is no reason for these excuses anymore. The answers are here, right now and at the present time. Your resistance to accept the truth will only hinder your Spiritual growth in the future, which could affect the final judgment that is part of your future. Be open to the change. Start the work of your soul! Start now and do not be late again.

Your resistance to learn now will hinder the growth that you really need at this time, to help your growing spirit, and this ailing World! Help God to help you.

God is calling you now, and He is revealing His own secrets, to help us with our difficult Human existence. These are simple steps to enlightenment, and God wants you to learn it, to be back to His fold and be closer to His Heart. He will guide you step by step Himself when you are ready to receive the gifts of wisdom!

Chapter 12
The Humble Servant

"It Is I, Oh Lord I Pray!"

Humbly I pray,
Before You, I have died..
Before You, I have cried...
And before You, I have thrived!
Humbly I Pray,
Homage I Pay!
Forgive me Lord I Pray, as my faith has a sway...
Here, I lay in the Hay of my humble Plea!

Humility in people is very hard to find nowadays. In this day and age, you observe other people around you and you will notice that nobody really cares to come down from their high horses and care about anybody or anything anymore. There is so much competition and jealousy. This World has become too cold to touch. These are true manifestations of immature Spirits in action. Our young generation, who are supposed to be the hope of the future, seemed to be lost and hopeless themselves.

This situation is very common everywhere now. We have lost our young generation to the very pit of our so-called progress. They are almost stripped with the foundation that is very necessary in their lives. We have already removed God from the basic learning foundation of the young. As parents, we are now almost powerless to discipline our young ones in the present time. And what we have called as progress is questionable, considering the fact that we do not clearly see the direction of such ideal progress in our lives and in the lives of our children.

As we fail to focus in our essence and our real purpose in life, we have also undermined the right choice to lead us to such progress. Along the way to our "so-called progress", we have also lost God's bright Light to help us see our path. God is now almost absent in our daily walks with life! Most men have already been misdirected themselves. Their concept of progress is to become so highly scientific and attain Science without God.

With God in the backburners of our lives, we have not become humbled servants to Him in our quest of scientific progress! The technical and scientific progress that man have developed and have been so proud of, have been also the detrimental factors that hindered the young generation's foundation to start their future in the right direction, because such quest was also without partnering with God.

The young generation is forced to evolve into their own empty direction; because they were not taught right on the right virtues and morality to consider that could have anchored them properly in their journey of life! Men have not been good examples of the young generation to follow.

At the present time, we continue to evolve into the emptiness of our lives and our direction to nothingness. We have lost ourselves into this wrong quest somehow. We have attained nothing but pride in our wrong accomplishments in life. A pride that will be a detrimental factor in our own individual spiritual health! Until we do something right now, we will be lost to oblivion and failures that could only hurt our children and us in the end! There is hope, and it is here right now. Regardless of your intelligent scientific mind, surrender to your loving Creator and ask Him to redirect your intelligence and science to help you discover the truth of things that is beyond you.

There is such a thing as intelligence on a different level that is beyond this scientific World. God's intelligence is beyond you and your science to comprehend, but with a little effort from you and I, we can sure be given the chance to explore so many possibilities with His help. Study only those areas of things and those avenues in your life that will matter to you and God most and that science, which will preserve and save the integrity of your Spirit. Areas of studies that will make you worthy in God's eyes, so you will have a complete and fulfilled answers to your life!

This is the direction that you should goal for yourself and your loved ones in the future, and arrive with the complete answers to your Spiritual journey! Be aware that a true and humble servant starts from within you! Study the simple truth about the existence of Human life and the breathing and living Human beings.

As you look around you, you can actually see people's faces and eyes, they only show a little glimmer of light and hope from their burdened spirits in different levels. If God will gift you, you will see through the eyes of every living Human being, and the work of their individual souls. You also will be able to differentiate the level of their Spiritual growth.

The eyes will truly give you the window to their souls and will help you see and determine the quality of life that they carry. Yes indeed, you will be surprised with the difference that you will see when you study the glow of the energy, emanating from an individual when you will have a gift of discernment.

You can actually choose the right people with the positive energy versus those that is without! I will give you a simple lesson of discernment in a given situation. If you see an arrogant person for example, observe him based on his behavior, speech, actions, the contents of his language, is it full of vile language, hatred and prejudice? Then, look at his eyes, (was it a very mean eye?) his face, (even if this man has some fine soft features, his looks will be replaced by a hard looking face and very mean expression.

This is because his very immature Spirit is crying out for help from the outside. Then, look at him again, and see the color of any light or aura that is emanating from within him. You will notice that he will seem darker in the light that he exudes, because his spirit cannot glow within, it is buried and hungry inside. It is like a candle that is now flickering with a little light, because it is almost ready to die!

Probably now, you can discern why people sometimes look so ugly, when outwardly they think they look so pretty, in their own superficial way of thinking, then they are so! It is a very sad fact that how we looked at beauty nowadays is totally different than how we look at it in the past. To the many of us in the present time, what is beautiful is only skin deep. Our very shallow way of thinking is reflected obviously in the way we think about life in a very physical and superficial way.

We have actually simplified everything according to our very ignorant views. We have also downgraded our intellect with the help of our arrogance and stagnated spiritual growth! Arrogance as the opposite of humility has been the total enemy of the Human Spirit in dire need of growth! You are what you have become. You will reflect what you have been doing. And it will show through you. As you do the negative actions in your life, you will also attract the most negative of situations for you.

It is an option and you have chosen it. Your freewill was just abused for the moment, but it had been used also to the detriment of your Spiritual health! If you do, do not complain why God did that to you…it was your own doing! You have become an ugly person because of your ugly actions! On the other hand, beauty does exist for good reason. Beauty also lies in the eyes of the beholder.

You can always find so much beauty in this World in so many varied forms of life, if you only knew how to discern it properly. With the proper exercise of humility in your everyday walk, you can surely gain the wisdom to see all kinds of beauty on this World. When you are not judgmental, you can start to appreciate the little packages of God's miracles presented before your very eyes, and you can be guided to discern the ways of looking at your life the right way. From the beginning of our lessons, God's tools of alignment cannot be used by anybody who has pride existing in that individual's heart.

You cannot be the master of anything unless you know how to follow the rules of good things. And unfortunately, I cannot just emphasize enough that there is no getting around the basic steps of the Eternal Tools of Alignment with God first!

God ask you to empty yourself before Him, and before He can even work on you. If you leave no room for Him to work, then He will not be there. It will just show Him, that you are not ready. Readiness in the walk will entail a lot of work and a serious one on your part! If you cannot even begin to clean house for God, He will not be there. God will never dwell in your dirty house. He is not a God of filth! Then don't even give any commitment to Him. A humble servant, cleans his house, prepares a feast for others and is not expected to disobey. There is no room for arrogance, when he is in his master's house. He will respect and obey the right orders, but should also question the wrong ones.

In your present life, God has also asks you to exercise profound humility. He cannot work on an almost full vessel. There is not just enough room to fill anymore, if you are halfway full. Ask yourself the question if you are ready to serve Him.

With the evolution of the Spirit for God, The mature Human Being now realizes that he or she does not exist anymore just for himself or for herself, but for other people too! His or her life now will have another meaning; which is to serve God and serve Him through His other children, in profound humility of all his or her actions!

Since he had already achieved the merits for his good deeds to the other children of God, he will continue to evolve and will continue to receive the grace of God in his life. His or her focus will be redirected outside of himself or herself. He now lives in total surrender and understand that no matter what, God will be there walking with him or her!

Now the focus becomes an objective one instead of a subjective one. He or she will now become detached from the lies and will only believe in the truth.

The discernment of the spirit will be so high in the level of an ordinary man, because he will not be ordinary anymore. He has become the favored child in God's watchful eyes. He or she will become conscious, that it is not about him or her anymore, but about other people aside from his or herself and his or her family. There will be a lot of emotions of love for other people other than his or her own. The humble servant will only follow the right command of his or her master in God. This servant is very strong in the spirit that the focus of her mentoring as life goes on becomes apparent in the way of his or her walk in life.

The reality is clearer at this time; for with his or her humble heart, things will be done in the calmness of love and devotion and the commitment to follow only God's direction! We as ordinary people will stay in the sideline and will observe them in silence. They will move around us in the silence of their devoted hearts! We will learn their ways of humility and peace. It will be a very humble beginning that will redirect us in our lives. In the end, we will forget the wants and the needs that we are used to, for we will be shown the way that God will provide for the rest!

The pride that we are accustomed to in the past will now be replaced with the quiet humility of the present. And the temporary needs and the wants will now become a blur vision of the past. For God's clearer visions through the work of the Holy Spirit will be dominant in our lives!

Chapter 13

Carry the Light

"Treasure Your Friends"

Always treasure, the moments shared.
Always remember, Pleasures spent.
Connect the Love, Connect the Peace.
Each moment shared, is shared with Grace!
Fond memories, Golden Years!
Life ever after, Joyful Place!
Gather your friends and treasure their space...
They are your miracles and you are theirs!
Praise time well spent... because
Friends are precious through the End!

    If we believe in God and surely there is no excuse anymore after you read the first book, we must now understand that we are responsible for all the misgivings that we have done on this Planet. God has given us a chance to redeem ourselves from the evils that have consciously or unconsciously used us. We are given the chance to start a new journey of faith and increase the strength of the spirit to help us endure the tests of our time. We are also given the knowledge that we have to slow down and simplify our lives, to prioritize only the things that we have to do in this journey. As we have expected God's wisdom and guidance, we are also expected to focus first on the things that will matter most in the salvation of our souls. God has been waiting for a good change from all of His children.

    He has been waiting for eternity from us to assure Him of our commitment to goodness and righteousness. But it really is up to us to use the gift of free will, to help us make the right decisions as we proceed with our individual lives. As we tread through with our journey of life, we must now include in our every action the work of our Spirit.

We must not refuse to help other people of God to walk the straight path with the lights and love that He has taught us. We have to stop, pause for a little while, and look around to find the areas of other people's life that will need help from us. Along the way, we will make a difference in other people's life, and help them to anchor themselves in the strength of God's loving ways.

We shall include taking the responsibility for every action that we take. We shall, and we must take some degree of responsibility, to heal this ailing World from all the evils of life and carry our individual lights to heal this Universe and ourselves! When we learn and practice the Eternal Tools of Alignment with God, our ways will change to comply only with God's wishes and instructions. And when used properly, it will help us with proper discernment to help us make the right choices, and make the right decisions. Cleansing will take effect in our ways of how we do things for good reasons and for good intentions. Along the way, it will help us cleanse not only our Physical self, as well as our Spiritual self; we will definitely feel the difference of our entire Spiritual health.

Carry the light of God in your hands and continue to shine its light and aim it to every dark corners of this Earth. Drive this World away from the presence of those little dark monsters that will try to thrive on the flesh of your brethren. Help drive away evil and ugliness from the face of this Earth! As you carry the Lights and Love of God in your dealings with your other brothers and sisters, continue to spread the wisdom of God's teachings in your heart, that is most needed at these times.

Do not mind carrying the burdens for other people at times, when they needed you the most. Show them the Spiritual strength that God has shown you. Help anchor the true Christian and the Godly foundations for the faint in spirits of your brothers and sisters. Show them and guide them the ways of love and compassion. The light is within you and around you. Let others tap into their inner individual lights, so they themselves can be examples of light for others too.

Help them grow with you in the Spirit of love, goodness and kindness. Encourage this very energy to dwell on the face of this planet. Lead the way for the change of direction. Lead your brothers and sisters in God, to the direction that is only going to the right path of Spiritual maturity that will prevail in this lifetime. Command the winds of change, and summon the waves of the ocean, to help each other realize a beautiful future reality of this Planet! Continue your walk in the Love and Lights. As if there is no more tomorrows, spread these love and lights in the name of God. Help erase the darkness of the past and of the present of these other people's lives, and in the future of the other children of God who still lives.

Live your lives to the fullest, without losing any day on unnecessary trivialities that will only slow you down. Make an honest commitment to yourself and to God first, and the rest will only fall into its place in due course of time!

As you walk your life in God's name, remember that your reward only awaits you in God's kingdom and let God do the rest for you. Do not falter in your faith, and do not encourage doubt to slow you down. Keep to your heart always of the seriousness of the true purpose of your life. And be aware of the signs of weakness in your Spirit. Be conscious of the ways of God, and let His ways dominate your every action, and your every word towards your fellow men. Have faith and do not waver in your belief and good judgments. You will grow in due time and in God's perfect timing.

Be patient in your walk, and be patient in your actions. As you carry the light of God, your patient and careful ways, will ultimately reward you with the wisdom of the Spirit to make it grow to its full potential in God. Your senses will be sharpened in every direction that you will take.

You will try to eliminate the noise of your life, because a little noise at this time will be unbearable. You wake up to a change that is imperative, to sustain your Spiritual health. In this lifetime, there will be no end to your continued quest for life and its answers. Bear in your heart and in your mind though, that the answers is within you and with God's guidance, you will be able to get all the answers that you may need and seek in the future. Our path to enlightenment does not begin right away. It will entail a lot of work on our part.

When things are done in good time and in the godliness of our very own actions, a change of positivism in our lives will happen. As we carry the light of God's awareness and love, we will surely be able to put back the bright and strong light of our now flickering candles of life! As a communal group of God fearing and God loving people, we will be the force to reckon with in the future. United we will grow in obedience to God. We will fear no evil, for God's armies will topple anything or anybody that will go against us for our Crusade for good. In the end, we will show that Love is the answer to every reason for life that we may encounter in our journey. Love is a vital presence, and the only ammunition that will answer and solve most problems in this World. If we can only maintain a minimal observance of goodwill one day at a time, then we can grow properly in good faith. Save a soul one day at a time, and help grow a Spirit also, one day at a time! It will start within us first and foremost, and will spread to light the way to those who are lost and hopeless.

At this point, the path of renewal is open to you. This is the time to surrender your confused Spirit, so you will learn to forgive yourself and your past misgivings. You will also welcome the light of hope for a fresh start in life!

To remember the basic step of the Human element of Life is to remember the path of renewing the walk back to God. Obey God and He will be there to guide you back to your predestined life! As you carry God's torch, let go of this miserable World into the loving hands of its Creator, and pray for it to heal in its due course of time. Somewhere out there, Eternal Life will be waiting at last and the Eternal Flame of light will shine its way to our hearts!

Chapter 14

The Strength From Within

> **Twilight comes,**
> **Morning mourns,**
> **Deep as the Ocean,**
> **Bright as the Sun!**
> **Blind me with obedience,**
> **Shower me with delight,**
> **As I carry now,**
> **Your torch of Life!**

The power of any Human Strength is not solely based on the physical nature of man himself, but in his Spiritual growth and maturity. The strength is within this man! It is a part of an innate and complex creation of God! The strength of any man will enable him to adjust and to help him endure the right way in this worldly existence. He will be fully armed with the tools of love and the Eternal style that is only exclusive from God Himself! The Spiritual strength is that which God has endowed us to use and grow to its fullest potential in our lives.

The Spiritual strength of human life is the basis of how we grow in the highest level of our existence in this planet. In the present time and in this generation, we tend to focus on the Material side and the Physical side of our existence. We have focused our determination and attention to the accumulation of more money, more houses, more cars etc. It now about the status we are holding in our society, in terms of the material superficialities in life! We are never satisfied in our quest for more material accumulation.

Meanwhile, we have surrendered to the wrong priorities that may have kept us busy and have kept us lost from the center, that we need to follow. On the other hand, we have tried our hardest to build our muscles to satisfy our misconception that by maintaining all this superficial material wants and physical desires, we will be able to achieve our so called high social status in life. In real life, we have become so busy trying to build a Castle in the air. This Castle has a very unstable foundation and shelter for our growing souls. This is the Castle that could only deny us and divert from to the real Heavenly Castle that is waiting for us for a long time.

The strength in our Spirits will redirect us back to the fold. As we have something to turn in the form of our growing Spirits, now in God's direction and wisdom, our growing Spirits will enlighten us back to the right paths in the practice of our lives. The strength has always been within us, and that is the strength of our souls, who have grown to be mature Spirits for God!

As all the material and the physical things will rot in the end, the Spirit will live forever to go back to God! The pressure of life and the living in it matters so much in this everyday life. The mature Spirit has the proper means of discernment and wisdom, to make the right judgment call, per incident of Human living. And if at all everything will fail, it will be our strong Spirits that will carry us through all kinds of Earthly battles in time!

Without the proper growth of the Human Spirit, man's life would be noisy and a chaotic one. Every decision will be a confusing signal, to either make the right or wrong move. Whether the decision will be made right away or later, will still be the same outcome every time in the midst of confusion! But a strong Spirit will always have the wisdom and the possible answers to help straighten and enlighten a confused soul!

The strength of the Spirit is not just an outward manifestation in the Physical form of the Human display but rather, in the actual Spiritual display that is internally manifested. This internal manifestation can always be shown outwardly on how Man reacts to a given situation. May it be to the direction of a physical or mental exercise of life, the Strong Spirit will open the door to the wisdom of truth to help save the Man.

The way that a man acts or makes his decision that is based in a situation presented upon him, will clearly define his internal strength through the making of the right judgment call, that is also equally a mature one. Maturity of the Spirit will carry with it the wisdom of enlightenment always that will always be a part of his growing process. Every human being has his weaknesses and strengths. The balance of both is essential to have a balanced way of life. As good and evil co-exists, so do positive and negative options that are open essentially to help develop such balance. A desire for a positive outcome in life is always an indication of a growing Spirit who is willing to change for the better. Sound decision- making is always desirable.

When God created man in His image and likeness, God has already blessed man the abilities and the tremendous capabilities of so much gift potential, and the power from God, to develop himself to be a godly person. The question is would this alone make man a most powerful creature of God? The answer is yes and no! Why is it?

Well, first of all we must consider where we are coming from. Originally in our very first Human existence, we have already failed to be who we are really by failing to use our Godly rights the proper way by disobeying God. Secondly, because of all the disobedience and the stubbornness that we are, we have not mature spiritually enough to understand the proper depth of our Human existence and purpose. But we still have a chance to change ourselves and grow our spirits properly. This is the reason that we must continually strive to grow and do the right thing as ever in the way we handle our lives.

We must consciously strive to continue to be the more compassionate and loving people, to put God more in our lives and show the World, that God's ways are the best ways to deal with life, and our everyday Human Existence properly.

When we fulfill God's plans for us on this Earth, God will surely be manifested in the way we live and conduct ourselves to the rest of His children. The Spirit that is within us can be unleashed to continue to spread love, compassion, and kindness to heal this ailing World of confusion and greed. As people of God, we will display the peace in our hearts and the loving nature of God's ways for the brotherhood of all of mankind.

To understand Spiritual strength is to understand God's strength for God will dwell in you, in your life, and in all of the people that surrounds you. Peace indeed will be experienced for all of mankind. In the future, we will be saved and we will be saving some people, one soul at a time.

In the future, once you are presented with any battles in your life, your inner Spiritual strength and energy will dominate and it will be the force that will shed the light in the times of your personal trouble and in your darkest hour of need.

The Spirit within you will be ultimately tapped and will be the power that is needed to assist you to win every battle in your life. Once a strong Spirit is achieved, one man's life is one man's power. You will reach the maximum discernment, Physically and Spiritually. You will be able to handle the battles of life itself and still be the strongest soldiers of your Eternal Father in Heaven. Nothing can deter you from walking the life of Jesus Christ; a life of profound humility and wisdom. You will have the wisdom and the ammunition of Love to rule your life.

Ultimately, the Spirit from within is the strongest force that we have to work harder to nurture to grow to be that ultimate Spirit that God can use to be a vessel ready to accommodate the whole universe of wisdom.

Love and peace will again reign in your life and you will be able to withstand any test that is humanly possible on this Planet. To be able to accommodate God's Spirit in your sanctified body should be the ultimate goal of the entire Human Existence of mankind. Receive the Holy Spirit to uplift your life. It is a privilege that we must honor and respect. Just because we are made in the image and likeness of God, does not give us the right to demand the automatic rights to receive all of God's gifts without working to deserve it.

God is a fair and a loving Father to all, although we are given the opportunity to receive Him and His messages equally, we still have to keep in mind that if we live our lives without God, our Godless lives will be an empty and hollow vessel for God to work on. Our constant and conscious refusal for Him to be in our lives has always been the outcome of how we have lived our lives. The more ignorant and proud we are, the more we alienate God from working with our Spiritual growth and us.

As I have said previously, we must always be aware of what we do and what we think, for we can be obviously judged on whether we have or we are without God in the end.

The Spirit will live forever to be with God. As our Earthly lives end, our beginning Spiritual life will also begin with God. We have to be ready on Earth, when the time will come when our Heavenly Father will claim us all back to His fold. Your end will be God's beginning! Please be aware that today's reality will not be the future's reality. What you think today will not be what will be in the future.

Ultimately, God will claim back your borrowed soul. Grow it properly to deserve all the chances of well-deserved merits for your whole entire Human Existence.

Never ever forget that we are all in a borrowed existence. A temporal existence! Our future permanent existence is to be with our Eternal Father. Use all the Eternal Tools of Alignment, and enjoy the ride to a more meaningful and eventful walk with God on Earth.

Chapter 15
The Fight From The External Forces

Life's Every Moment
Every moment of tears,
Every ounce of despair,
Every love to share,
Every freedom to bear,
Every time I dare,
To care for you and stare,
The noise so bad I hear,
Is thunder to my ears, I fear!
Spinning every moment,
Twirling every hour,
Life's hopeful moments,
Are every moment of Peace and Grace!

As you grow more in the Spirit, you will become more and more aware of your total surroundings. You will become very sensitive to energy. This time you will realize that almost everything on this Planet works on energy. With your newly acquired internal peace, you will become too sensitive to the noise around you. Now, you are as if going through your baby steps of an amazing reality. Waking up to a new knowledge and wisdom. You will be changed and you will become a sensitive person. As if reborn for a new life!

You then will be a new you. As if you have never lived before, you will have a new zest for life, and a compassion that you have never before felt in your heart. You will also experience the changes in how you look at things the way that is so different on how you were accustomed to. In your present life, these changes are vital to make a fresh start in your daily walks of life. There will be other influences and events that will totally catch you in some unexpected manner and direction.

People and changes in things that used not to matter or to bother you will also start to affect you in a different manner that you have never experienced before. The above changes are necessary to further your Spiritual growth. This is almost like a continued training phase that you will inevitably have to go through to be able to balance your way of life!

There will be an inevitable fight that will occur in your life from the external forces that surrounds you. And it will be more obvious for you at this time of your growth, because of your acquired sensitivity to energy. Another aspect of this change will redirect you to the discernment phase, in which you will learn to discern matters properly in its simplest to complex form and as you grow, you will rightfully attain the higher level of growth necessary to place you to the next level. You may wonder why you have to go through these different levels of growth?

Why not just give you everything, so it will be over and be done with? Well, unfortunately, in your humble state, God with His infinite wisdom and knowledge will only give you the gifts in the level that you can handle. With God's vast knowledge and infinite wisdom, it will be impossible for Him to just pour it all to any man on this planet. There is no such thing.

There is no perfect Spiritual man on this Planet that can accommodate any of God's wisdom by personal will, but it can be done only by God's will! Once God opens the door to learning, He will also open another door. In that hidden place, where there will be darkness that has existed, you will be allowed to peek into it the same as part of your training level, which is the Spiritual discernment. This door although, somewhere forbidden for most people to even peek, is sometimes allowed to a more matured and already trained Spirit that has accepted God totally and has already used the Eternal Tools of Alignment and one who has already received the gifts of wisdom. You will not be allowed this level of training, where you will have to discern the most dangerous of the other reality, which is the existence of evil and his cohorts if you are not ready to discern in the higher level of Spiritual maturity.

This is a reality that is so strong that if you are still weak in your faith and in your practice with life and have not even spread God's love to your brethren, you can be used and can be fooled without knowing it. This is the external force that you do not want to meddle with. You will not be able to challenge darkness, if you do not carry a strong beam of Light from God Himself. You will fall and get hurt if you do. And this is a fight that you must be ready in your life! And this is the fight that you have to be strongly determined to win at all times. The fight from the external forces of your life can either go Physical and Spiritual. The most dangerous fight of course is the Spiritual fight, because it will challenge your strong Spirit to no end. This is a fight that will continually keep on going while you are going through tremendous levels of learning to strengthen your own Spiritual walk.

On Earth, while you are trying to spread the lights and the love of God, the prince of the darkness will continue to challenge you spiritually, and will try to intimidate you from fulfilling your Spiritual Mission. He will stop you at any cost or by any means possible, to spite God and your work for God.

The only possible means to fight back effectively against the challenges of a Spiritual nature is to align yourself with God and to use His Eternal Tools to the utmost, especially one of His Eternal gift in particular, which is the gift of the Discernment of the Holy Ghost or Spirit. This higher level of this particular Spiritual gift is a very vital factor in the fight against the external forces of darkness! The most difficult fight that you will ever fight in this lifetime is a fight against the vile presence of evil, and to be able to win against the force of darkness, that is now spreading in this planet and is gaining edge on this Planet.

This is the biggest fight that God would want us to win in the end. He has prepared all His Eternal Tools and Ammunitions through the power of His Love and Energy of God's Holy Spirit, to win against the darkness of our lives. So as God continue to endow you with all the necessary Eternal Gifts for your salvation and protection, play your part in return, and play it like you deserve to receive such gifts.

Receive your gifts and be responsibly gifted, and act on the expectations that are only good, to maintain your Spiritual Health! The changes will be a tremendous one in the right time of your life and in God's perfect timing. When your five senses will become six or more, do not be alarmed. Just know that when you are doing the right things always in the name of God, He is continually working in your favor, and He will continually add more things unto you.

He will bless you with ordinary and extra ordinary gifts that can be handled by your expanded and growing Spirit. He will not ever give you what you cannot handle. God always wanted you to have the power to discern, and the power to fight and choose the right battles to win. In your Spiritual development, you will now notice areas in your life that you have not paid attention before.

Your heart will now experience feelings of deep love and compassion, for yourself and for others. New awareness will now be an important part of your life. The idle mind that you have not used before will now be as active as you want it to be. You will become the gift to yourself, and a gifted Human Being to another. This time you have truly received the Spirit of God working in your life.

With the right mind, body and spirit, this time you are more than ready to face the World and more than ready, to live your life to the utmost. A new reality in the same World! Slowly your vigor will be renewed, and your ways will inevitably change.

It will not be the same anymore and a renewed person manifest itself for all to see. As your internal peace continues, you will lose the line of living an agonizing life. You will rule your decisions in the wisdom of God. Your friends will be magnified instead of your enemies. You are living in your Paradise on Earth! An amazing realization of a new reality indeed!

By now, you would think your work is done! My dear friends, no! You are just in your beginning journey of enlightenment! And I wish you good luck in your walk with God! Receiving a few gifts from God is not enough! You are just getting ready to receive more. Remember God has infinite gifts that He will shower you up to what level that you can take. God is perfect and to have a beginning journey to almost perfection with Him is not accomplished that quick and that easy. Although your Physical capabilities can handle a lot, it is only your Spirit that can magnify to receive all of God's gifts.

You will definitely overwhelm your physical and mental capabilities by just a mere gesture of God waving a hand at you because it is only the Spirit, your Higher Self, that can totally accommodate God's graces in your borrowed lifetime.

When God opens His door to you; the walk of life will also be a little harder. The new awareness that you just have experienced will also open a new reality, that for the years of living your life, you have tried to disregard as a non- existent reality. As the saying goes, ignorance is not an excuse; it has never been an excuse to do things in the proper way of our individual walk on this Planet. There is indeed another existence and another reality that we must recognize to accept and recognize to avoid.

There is indeed another force in this Earthly existence that is allowed to have a part in the everyday discernment and decision making that we make. This reality is a strong force that deters us from our straight-line walk with our Eternal Father. This is another harsh reality that although we are not ready to accept, is inevitably part of our borrowed existence. There is the truth of the existing reality of a Defied Spiritual being from God. This force is as strong almost as of God's energy that is continually forcing us to do what is ungodly. It has defied God Himself because it is a strong energy that is without God and is also full of jealousy and pride. The energy that is not of God's is a strong force to reckon with.

This particular energy devours any possible borrowed soul on Earth, for He also claims He is the father of this World, and claims all Human Beings as his prey to spite God. When he uses you, he will confuse you with a false promise of Glory.

The end product of his teachings will be confusion, hatred and anger. Beware of his presence working in your life, and be conscious not to open any door to welcome him in your actions. The path to your destruction is the product of his dark influence in your life. Any used souls by this energy, will be a confused soul! This is an infinite entity that is allowed to have a little part of Human existence and spread its disturbance in order to confuse mankind and to spite our Eternal Heavenly Father. It co-exists in your spiritual fight for right or wrong. It will spread hate for our God, who is the total embodiment of Love.

He will do exactly what is the opposite of God's nature. This entity uses hate versus love; negative energy versus the positive energy, uses pain versus happiness, and thrives best at your pain versus your happiness! This is a total negative energy. When it uses anybody or anything, it will show itself as a knight in shining armor with only the intention of deception.

Whenever it devours and uses a soul in a Human Being, it comes so subtle and so powerful, that it will be very hard to discern it without the proper discernment from the gifts of God. This is the reason why we must recognize the duality of our body and soul, and the existence between Good versus Evil. God will be there to shower us with the right wisdom and discernment of the Holy Ghost to aid and protect us from this very dangerous battle that you will inevitably face from time to time.

This is the fight from the external forces! We must be ready to address this reality at all times for our good, and for our own protection. A reality that although we have tried to undermine, is a reality that is not going to go away that easy. It is present in this lifetime of Earth and you are a vital part of it! Be aware and be vigilant to protect yourself and your loved ones.

Let us all accept and eventually be ready to fight the external Spiritual forces that will be presented to us as we tread though life. But understand that we cannot do this particular battle alone without God's help.

Be aware that the powerful Angels of God have defeated this entity in the past, and we are but unfortunately, too weak to battle it personally without God's help.

Fortunately, in this book, God has given us a chance to use His Eternal Tools of Alignment to be the ultimate winner and warrior for Him, if we just follow His guidance and nurturing, we will grow our Spirits to battle and win against it.

We must continue to close the door so as not to permit the presence of this entity's negative energy to bother us and confuse us. We must not allow even a minute for this opportunistic and troublesome energy to deter us from living a Christ-like existence for our Eternal Heavenly Father. Always carry your faith in God like a torch of flaming love to obey and follow His Golden rules of Human Existence. Unwavering faith is needed in these trying times of Human Existence and change.

Be humble to recognize your strength to grow your spirit and in your weaknesses, ask God for help. Let Him shower you with the discernment that we need at all times. Again, it is your personal energy and God's love that will rule this World. Make a difference and be strong to ultimately defy the strongest negative energy that will deter you in your true quest for life.

When you carry love in your heart and the compassion for God's other children, you will not only help create a peaceful World, but you will also become the vessel that God can bless to clean all unwanted negative forces that can be seen or unseen. When God gifts you, your mere presence will eliminate the negative forces that will protect other children of God and will drive other presence of unwelcome forces. You will carry God's light and help with the enlightenment of this World.

You will also be the power that rules your World in the most righteous way. So go and be God's role model by example, and spread the good news! I am wishing that you would grow your spirit in the end to win all the battles that you have chosen against the powerful external force of darkness!

Chapter 16

Discernment By The Holy Ghost

"The Eternal Tools"

**God blessed us with the Tools of Strength!
In our Struggles of Life, and
In the Despair of Our Existence,
In the moment of sorrow, there is Joy!
In the moment of chaos, there is Peace!
In the moment of despair, there is Hope!
Look forward to Life, and
Live full of Love,
Look forward to the Light, because in here is your
chance to experience God in your Heart, for here comes…The
Eternal Tools to guide your Eternal Way to Life!**

The gift of discernment by the Holy Ghost will be the most profound of all your spiritual experiences. Here, the power of the Holy Ghost is felt within the growing Spirit of man. It will dwell within him and it will be a very powerful influence that will help his Spirit grow in the right direction. With the absence of the Holy Ghost or the Holy Spirit, as we call it in our modern times, our journey in life, will be weak and empty. With the absence of proper discernment, it will be very difficult to make the right move and to make the right choices in life. Living this life is already a difficult journey for a lot of us, and the ways of this World, have downgraded our Spirits into the nothingness and the emptiness that we do not deserve. As we hang on to our dear life, we knew down deep in our hearts that we truly needed the help of our God above!

In the midst of the darkness on this Planet, we all need the light and the guidance to redirect our lost journeys. In the future of our lives, when we have to retrace our steps, we will have a difficult path, if we cannot even see where we are going! We have to discern now the facts of our lives and the right direction of our sojourn of life! Although we are made in the image and likeness of our Creator Himself, and we are armed with His gifts and His innate Light to help us in our adventures in life, we still have to grow our talents and our abilities in conformity with God's wishes. With obedience to God's rules, we will grow our Spirits properly, to be able to attain the wisdom and the discernment of the Holy Ghost to guide our daily walks of life.

Part of our growth, is to be able to grow ourselves with the discernment that is only given to us by God's own Holy Spirit at work in our individual lives. The balance on how we have to play our role on this planet cannot be achieved properly, if we do not acquire the wisdom of Discernment from God's own Spirit. This gift alone is of the highest level, if we could have attained it in our time, and before our future transformation event. The daily walks that we take each day, will somehow present real events that will be very difficult for us to discern in the future, but it is sometimes allowed to train our innate discerning abilities, that we will need to mature and to aid us, in the daily decision-making that we may have to undertake. The discernment of the Holy Ghost is a must Eternal Tool that we needed desperately at these times, of our present Spiritual World situation ad the future Spiritual warfare that is about to happen in the future.

The last few years of our lives, have been the toughest to most of us who are just trying to survive our daily lives. The state of confusion and chaos has changed the outlook of this World forever! We fear for what is the inevitable event. We are presented with numerous options and changes that have battled our spiritual strength to the utmost! In the present time, if man is not careful, he will be forced to face an ultimate destruction of his Spirit. This present World has lost the essence of the real Spiritual life to the abyss of darkness. Man will have a hard time to recover what is lost in the future. Since we have not started the work of our very own soul to Spiritual maturity, it might be too late to start again and we might not be given another chance at it!

"In the future of your distant lives, only the strong in the spirit will survive."

This was revealed to me in one of my visions of Jesus Christ as He was saying it me directly as if I have to make it a very strong priority for my life!

In one vision with Mother Mary, she also said,

"In the future, your money will not hold its value anymore."

And then she continued saying,

"Only love will move your cars and will start your engines in the end."

Until now, I am still confused by what Mother Mary has said in the past. But with proper discernment of the Holy Ghost, what was said in the form of parables will have a very different meaning for you and me, depending on our own individual level of Spiritual maturity. We have to grow our Spirits now to almost perfection with God!

We have to prioritize this part of us, which is our highest form of our self. We have to expand our Spirits right at this moment to accommodate the vast wisdom of knowledge from God!

The profound spiritual manifestation and experience can be balanced off with a mature spirit, and the proper discernment of the Holy Ghost. With these Eternal gifts comes the Eternal Wisdom and Discernment! As we grow our Spirits, we shall receive the gifts that are very personal to our nature and to our Spiritual capacities. Anything less in the eyes of God will not be worthy of His attention. God has balanced our very own creation with the complexity of our being created Humans.

Human nature by itself has provided some of the complex Human needs. The experience that will stem from the work of the Holy Ghost will be a mystical and an almost magical one. For those individuals that are not ready to accept God in their individual lives, they will not be receiving the Holy Ghost miracles at any time. God and His Spiritual Messengers will not be significantly active for those who are non- believers, although other entities that are not from God may be significantly be active in an individual's life who does not have the strong in God. The big difference will be on how the interplay of this particular experience will affect a person's life and his faith.

God do not condone violence, hatred and pride with any of His teachings. Anything that carries the message of darkness, hatred, violence and prejudice will differentiate the message as an ungodly one! God teaches the lights and the love in every occasion in our lives and He abhors war, violence, hatred and prejudice! God does not thrive on any negativity on this World! It is not His ways, as He is a true embodiment of pure Love! If anyone does experience a highly mystical experience that is charge with any message of darkness, violence, hatred and pride, it is definitely not coming from God. Believe that any emotion that condones violence, hatred, war, and bloodshed are all the negative emotions that are coming from the eternal enemy of God. God is a total embodiment of love and peace.

All His teachings represent those that have presented ingredients of love, lights and peace. Do not be deceived by the wrong messages from the dark side that are always possible with the absence of the gift of Discernment by the Holy Ghost!

How you will be able to attain the gifts of discernment is totally up to you. But it takes commitment and hard work in your part to be able to earn it. As you strengthen your walk and resurrect your Spirit to grow, God will help you along the way. But you must carry the faith in your heart and gather your strength to continue the walk as far as you could go.

When the time comes, that you will receive your rewards to guide you in your daily life, trust in God to win for you the rest of the battles that you cannot do anymore in the future. During the times of your weakness, let God's Holy Spirit replenish the strength that you most needed at the moment.

The depth of any encounters and highly mystical experience can only be judged by how mature the Spirit can discern the source. The mature Spirit in God can properly achieve discernment of the source by using the gift of Discernment by the Holy Ghost. The proper discernment can only be achieved if one has matured his Spirit to be able to receive the gift and the wisdom of discernment. When we are ready to begin the discernment on any given experience, we can always start by praying to have the Holy Ghost be present within our hearts and in our minds to aid us in the proper discernment of things that are happening, and to properly discern the events that have been presented before us. Discernment of the Holy Ghost could sometimes automatically come to an already matured Spirit working his work for God.

It could come into the midst of any need at the moment or to any decision-making that has to be made. Discernment by the Holy Ghost at all times can be very deep, and can be a very unusually profound experience. It will require a very strong and mature Spirit of Man to welcome it that easy. Since it involves a Spiritual work of discernment, it will entail a total and very focused attention and energy to properly discern any circumstance or event that needs such discernment.

The Spiritual experience in itself will be a basis of proper Spiritual discernment. How, when, where, and what is received, and from what source it is coming from, are very important factors to consider in making the right discernment in a given time. Remember always that in this Planet, there will be a coexisting opposite forces that will continually bombard us with situations and events that will require our proper discernment.

With the help of the Holy Ghost, who is ever present within a grown Spirit of a Godly man, proper discernment will be possible and can be achieved immediately in a matter of Heaven's minutes! It is of immense importance that we know which direction we are going at all times! With our Spiritual growth and the proper discernment by the Holy Ghost, we will be opening more doors for the good of mankind to be able to endure the challenges of our time. It will be very hard to use the mental capacity, as it has a limited capability to recognize the experience that is based on the Spiritual phenomena.

But when one's Mind and Spirit are harmoniously working together using God's wisdom that has been blessed upon a man, it will become the most powerful tool and ammunition for protection against a life full of misery and despair. Although the Spirit World's reality is at arms length to our Physical reality, and as true as it exist, the proof cannot be measured by just mere physical proof. The reason is of course, it is not tangible enough to be easily measured and studied. To believe in our God that we have not seen is another mystery that we have to solve. Faith alone will not be enough to support any one's belief.

Sacrifice is also a part of the walk. Love from the very beginning is a must ingredient, and with the torch of life at least you may be ready to believe your true journey! With all the factors that I have mentioned above plus the discernment of the Holy Ghost, man will have all the powerful Eternal Tools and almost enough power to be in God's side as His warrior and humble servant to be examples of a bred of growing Spiritual men under God's name! Our ways is to believe of that which can be seen and tangible to prove. The most motivation that we use is to study only certain events in our life that we consider normal. Our limited understanding is the product of us not surrendering the control of our so-called reasoning and our intelligence over to God.

Our inequities have been magnified because we have continued to wallow in our very own ignorance and our continued failure to cede surrender for God to educate us with His wisdom. When you freely give God a chance to be in your life, God's gifts will also be flowing within you that you will ultimately transform you as His good servant with that certain look and light that is only coming from Him. You will also be able to discern good versus evil in an instant. And you will finally see this World and your life thru God's eyes. Making the right decision will be a snap because you can tap into the tremendous amount of wisdom that is available for the taking. In utilizing God's discernment, there will be no more questions, only answers.

The answers in your life will solve all the problems that had made it very difficult for you in your daily walk of life in the past. In the future, you can drive away the darkness of your life by shining the torch of God's bright, warm, and loving Light. With the hope of a new beginning and a fresh start, anticipate a great adventure with God! With God in your life, you will have a brighter future and you will walk with Him in true love! The discernment by the Holy Ghost is the most important tool that we must master in this lifetime. Proper use of discernment will aid and protect us from the most dreaded life of confusion.

Discernment of the Holy Ghost will also be essential for nurturing us in our Spiritual growth. Properly discerning the events in our lives will ultimately shield us from the evil that is so evident in this World. There has been a tremendous presence of strong spiritual forces in this World and we must be aware to recognize and differentiate it at anytime and anywhere in our lives.

There is an ongoing Spiritual warfare that is ongoing in the present time. We must adhere to the strict confidence that only the Holy Ghost can assure our Spirits of the revelation and the discernment in the right direction. With learning properly the tools of discernment, we will be in control of our visions and dreams. The wrong notions of things will not fool us. We will be stronger to fight the right battles in our life that will threaten our only Spiritual existence and growth before God's Eyes!

We will be able to discern and exercise restraints in our judgments and decision-making. The torch of light that is only coming from our ultimate Creator will guide us into the light and love of our days! The danger in our lives is always with the wrong discernment of our Spirits for we tend to believe what is unimportant and trivial. As our wrong notions and misconceptions slow us down, we are still given the chance at this time to renew our life. With the Eternal Tools of Alignment, we will together begin a new journey and hope for the discernment of the Holy Ghost to arrive timely in our lives! We have been weakened by the wrong priorities that stagnated the Spiritual growth that is needed at this time. It is very difficult to tap into our inner wisdom when there is almost a non-evidence of progress with the Spirits that we now have. Let us all hope that we can own the Spirit of God! Let it flow within us to guide us. It will protect us always from the danger of evil and misdirection. It will anchor us properly from the storms of deception.

The Holy Ghost will be the Shield of Ultimate protection from the big Evil that is about to disturb your peaceful existence in the future of this World. Stay away from the negative path of Spiritual destruction. Put in the positive flow of energy from the Source of your Creation.

Let it engulf and bless you with His guiding tool of discernment so you can learn how to slowly ease you pain. Your pain should have never existed in the first place anyway, if you just have the proper understanding of your life and the nature of your ways! Work harder in your Spiritual growth; it will be a force to reckon with In the future to reconcile your Spirit, with the Spirit of the Heavenly Father. Remember that the depth in understanding the growth of your Spirit will depend on your personal effort and hard work and know that in the end…your life will depend on it!

In this day and age, we have been bombarded with all kinds of information and negativities that will surely weaken, even the strongest of the Spirit of Man. And the reality of the time, has point us to confusion and misconception that the everyday life that we have has now become very difficult for most of us to even survive our daily walks in life!

If we do not even have the faith and the trust that God is in our midst, and will continually guide and protect us from the darkness of this life, we will be vulnerable victims to the wrong and bad things that are happening among us in this very planet. This is the time, that we must mature and grow our Spirits to enlighten our daily walks and help us sustain at least a healthy perspective in this lifetime. The time has come to really pay attention to the ways to make us sustain and keep a healthy Spirit for the sake of our very own future endeavors.

How we walk our life will affect the future that we have created in the present day. Our future in the end will truly depend on the strengths of our Spirits as our morals and virtues will deteriorate inevitably with time that is consistently changing in this World! The discernment of the Holy Ghost is a gift that man will have to strive harder to attain to face the realities that is about to happen in this World!

The mind alone will not be able to help in the proper discernment on the order of things in this World and the spiritual warfare that is ongoing that can or cannot be seen by the mere mortal sight. Life as complex as it is, is a product of a grand plan by its Creator that is God! To think less of its complexities will only stagnate our already dwarfed Spiritual progress.

Only your Spirits can expand to accommodate the vastness of the wisdom that can answer all our questions in this lifetime. Grow your spirits properly, and you will be blessed with the truth about your human existence!

Chapter 17

Mankind's Dominion Over Earth

"In The Midst of Summer"

**Silent Night,
Peaceful Kite,
Stir of Echoes,
Echoes of the Night!
Mermaids Talking,
Birds a Floating,
In the Midst of Summer, It is Twilight!**

At this point in your life, you have Spiritually grown and have duly acquired the highest wisdom that only God has given and endowed a special human being, which is you. You have now elevated your status in the eyes of God, because you are given the gifts and the wisdom of Life. And you have become His cherished child and a favored one in His side. You have properly aligned your life with your Creator. You are now the privileged spirit on this Earthly existence. You have become the super Human amongst all men alive! You have understood the gifts that are not to be abused. And have walked the walk of spreading God's love! You have become an example to boot, because your nature is not wild.

All along, your strength is not derived from this World, but from the out of Worldly energy that is only from the Heavenly Father! You have now also become the man of the Universe of love. You will walk to continue to weave the beads of wisdom and to spread the seeds of forgiveness. Your spiritual strength will not be a show for you, but will be a show to see in action of its positive mission. This time, you will not follow the path to the shallow and hollow greens masked by snow! And you will neither follow the common path of men nor make them the example of your actions, because deep inside you heart, you know that the street of destruction is never for you. **Your wisdom will be so deep. You will solve mysteries after mysteries of Life. You will also realize that gold lies beneath the golden halo of Time and Light to form the pearl of beauty and delight. The wisdom indeed is deep and the mysteries will abound but you are going to look forward to the work of your heart!**

Then, you will truly Love as you have never loved before. You have embraced the truth about Love, and you have understood that the same product of Love, applies to all of your Human dealings. This thing called Love will be a universal motivation for you to sustain the life of your Spiritual Existence. **You will continue to live for as long as the light of the day, to the fullest of everyday, that only tomorrow can end! As you put your feet forward, you are only hoping for the best that is only to come in your life. Live your life as if there will be no end!**

You have dominion boot and you have the grace of God to be a proud part of your daily walks in life! You will also acquire the wisdom to realize, that your life is only a product of time that will be harvested according to the will of God; and to how much quality it has attained. Do not abandon yourself not to the wolves, but to the sheep of good fortune! The dominion will be a forceful and a peaceful one, because you will exercise to use the message of Love. Surely, life will be an easier one to tread, because your dominion of life will prevail. Your ways will be strong until the end that God will take you back! And if you reach the ripeness of Life, there will for sure be a quality in your lifAs a quiet and fulfilled spirit, you will have learned to

It will be hard for others to resist not following your bliss! Your dominion in life will always caress the life of the people that you have touched in peace. You will have the control of your life in the quiet satisfaction of your good deeds and actions towards other people in your life! There will be peace to rule your heart. Your mind will now be free from the ignorance of the past. You will be endowed with the intellect of the wisdom that is only shared with God! With God, leading the way to your future, you will become the follower that you needed to be in His fold!

You follow His lead in utmost respect, reverence and honor to fulfill a mission that only you can understand! He will light your way with love. The future of your life will be a bright start, and a new beginning that is full of anticipation and of the wisdom of life! Together with God, you proceed to preach what has helped you attain that certain elusive wisdom from the past. Your present will be stronger, because at this point in your life, you have possessed the ammunition of love for your future! The dominion of your life will inevitably happen in this World! You have conquered your own fears, and have become stronger for the rest of your brothers and sisters. You will become the exemplary example of faith and wisdom, because you will show the World the real walk for God! With all the blessings that are only coming from God, you will walk this Earth with a steadfastness and singleness of purpose that is only personal to you!

You have truly become **One with God** and you have become the true example of a human servant at best.

" **When the rest of God's creations will follow your example, on this planet, war and hatred will slowly disappear. The core of their lives will be built in the foundation of Love!"**

Love will rule in each other's life, as peace will then be again reestablished, for this World! Together we will be blessed in this World, with love and peace! Mankind's dominion on this planet will be a good future reality, for then, a man will become the intelligent follower of God. He will rule his life with the wisdom of the truth of all the realities in his life that will be before him.

He will not be easily weakened by misgivings and pride. And he will not easily succumb to anger and hatred that will stain his life! He will be able to control not only his emotional life, but also, his mental, physical and spiritual life! Man will dominate this planet in the almost perfection and obedience to God! And peace at last will last, for all of the Earth's inhabitants! As we dwell in peace and in love, we will be truly blessed with the grace of God! The abundance of our lives will start to manifest before our very own eyes!

We will be more organized in our ways and better in our deeds to the rest of the people of God! God will also dwell in the midst of our lives! He will continue to work on the Spirits of the lowly and the poor, and He will continue to protect and strengthen them in their daily walks of life! This will be an ultimate life of man, where he can walk, without the fear of the shadow of death behind his back. And peace at last will also rule in his life! As man continue to walk in the good graces of God, his Spirit will mature to attain the highest wisdom of his life to support his weakness and inequities in dealing with his everyday journey. The piece of this planet will be ready for him to dominate.

Man will become the ultimate strength to rule in God's behalf. If only he knew that he is truly indeed one, in his Spirit with God! He then, will not have the fear of living life! He will continue his stride in the magnificent ways from God. His wisdom attained will make him glow in the darkest point of his life! Man will truly discern a good future for his family, his neighbors and his friends. He will proclaim to own, only a little piece of what will make him sustain the pieces of his life!

He will continue to be grounded in humility and be at peace for the rest of his life. If only we can lead as true leaders of men, this time will be the moment of truth! Because when a man matures as the Spirit of God, he will truly lead with the wisdom of the Light and Love of God.

Chapter 18

The Quiet And Fulfilled Spirit

"Come Holy Spirit, let the World thrive only for God!"

"The Bygone Years"

Seconds of Time,
Minutes of Struggles,
Hour after hour, time of tomorrow!
Morning Mists, Evening Stars!
Sun Rays of Fortune,
Wishing Stars of hope!
Glitters of Gold,
Pearls of Wisdom,
The Bygone Years of Today... is Tomorrows Hope!

A quiet and a fulfilled spirit of man has learned the wisdom and the peace from God! He will live a long life of bliss and grace, because he is a man of God! He has weathered the storms of his life by using the Eternal Tools of Alignment. He will share the peace that emanates from within him. He will walk his daily life in peace and in the warmth of love and of forgiveness. A spiritual vessel that has accomplished the best ways of life, deep enough to strengthen his once lost life! He will be oblivious to the chaos of this World, because he has focused his attention to the most important facts of life.

He has properly put things in the order of importance to his life and to his family and friends. He will walk in profound humility to be an example for other people to follow.

He is now the ultimate man on Earth! With peace in his spirit, and a fulfillment of his needs, he has attained the highest wisdom and satisfaction in the end. He will continue his stride in an anticipation of great adventures in peace and love. His World will not be in chaos, because he will refuse to go near the noise that a man creates for himself!

He will not dwell in a negative environment and will not condone the deeds of his heartless neighbors. He is determined to live in peace for his family and his neighbors. He does love himself and God enough, to avoid the dark traps of life! When a man truly attains the highest wisdom of his mind and of his spirit, then peace will rule his heart!

His dominion in his lifetime will be a promised fulfilled. He will walk his daily life with the peace and love that he truly wants to share to all that will happen in his life! He will have attained his ultimate Peace! Peace at last will rule his heart and his life forever! He will have finally commended everyone who is righteous and have learned not to mock the gracious! Almost a perfected Human Spirit in a man – and that is you! You have understood that the perfection of the Human Spirit can be possible first by redirecting his goals towards the total abandonment of the material accumulation and aligns Himself directly with God!

And the knowledge that if, the material accumulation will deter his growth, he will abandon such in lieu of fulfilling the service for God! As God will come first in his life, God in return, will reward him with His Eternal Tools to aid him with his life! The knowledge alone that had kept your peace within yourself must be treasured. The focus now has been shifted to the right direction of your life, and your priorities will be all in order! Now, you have become the Shepherd of your Heavenly Father in Heaven! With true devotion and commitment, you will attend to His flock in total obedience and love. Deep in your heart you knew that, soon enough, God would only be harvesting the flock that is only quality and you are one of them! You have humbly surrendered your life on God's hands at this point in your life. You have now accepted the fact that no matter how much you want to control everything and anything in your life, there are things that cannot be changed or controlled no matter what you do. And the rest, you leave them all to God!

A quiet and peaceful Spirit is within you. A very fulfilled Spirit of God, for God is your ultimate Love. You also have acquired the wisdom that God has completed you and your whole existence. So now, you can hold your head up so high, because you can look beyond with a different look at life and the people around you. And this time you will have a much better attitude about your life! There will be a renewed feeling of inspiration to live life again with a much more anticipated joy and energy! An inspiration, that this will be a different time to start life in a new light and in a new beginning! A peaceful and a quiet Spirit! Only working in conformity with God's wishes and in following only His commandments. As if you have never lived this way before, you will continue to grace this World with you loving presence that is important to God! A quiet surrender to God's graces is now your way of life! You have a fulfilled and a quiet spirit for all to see. In your midst, people will find peace! In your charity, people will find love at last!

As you continue your journey with life, your quiet and fulfilled spirit will raise the consciousness of those who are in doubt. They will follow your lead, to be an example of their own true lives. The truth will simply come out through how other will see your life, because your spirit at peace will be strong to overshadow the anger when you are in a stride! There will be goodwill amongst the men of God! Peace will reign all the way to the skies up above. The true wisdom for man has finally arrived, in the life that is truly God's! You have become one with God in its true and wonderful oneness that is such a profound experience that is unique for you. As if for the first time, you have attained a level of growth that has breath into you a fresh perspective of your life! Your direction is clearer and your walk more meaningful.

As you formed a formidable alliance with God up above, you have also now become stronger in your spiritual dealings with your neighbors below. It has been an awakening experience of your life that saved you from the destruction of your very soul! As you tread your life in fulfillment of your mission, you have become strong and firm in your actions and in the way you deal with the World as a whole. Nothing can topple your spiritual strength and you anchor yourself firmly on the ground!

This is the ultimate goal of mankind. Oneness in Spirit with God's Spirit, and be in loving relationship with God. Everything that you have learned in life is a lesson in love and in building a unique relationship with God. And a quiet and fulfilled Spirit would have been your famous work of art. Together in your walk with God, you pledge only to serve and love Him. In return, He will have given you the unbelievable feeling of enlightenment and protection that only you can experience with Him. This time, you have achieved a very triumphant battle. Alas! You have finally listened. A quiet and a fulfilled Spirits of Human Beings will have mastered the tools of Alignment with God.

He or she could have found the secret of living a peaceful and a fulfilled life having acquired the wisdom that was gained from his own life experiences. Coupled with the acquired spiritual gifts that God Himself have bestowed upon Him, he could have attained the peace that was once very elusive in his life. As he continues to live his life, he will master the dominion of his life, in total peace and in the quietness of his Spirit. As evident in the way that he will live his life, he will not be deterred and be slowed down by the misgivings of this world. He will continue to shine his very own light in the midst of the darkness of this World!

There is no such thing as a complicated lesson in life. With God everything is simple and uncomplicated as long as you have acquired the wisdom that He already have bestowed upon you since the day of His creation of this World and you! God has created you in his image and likeness and bless you the gifts and sustenance to help you in this lifetime. Believe that you will have peace and love around you! If there is no one else He is always there for you!

A peaceful world is now achieved at this stage. Forgiveness will be common. There will be neither enemies nor weapons to fight war. This is achievable and not impossible.

Let the positive change happen in this World and let it start with you. Show the gifts that that you have gained and teach them the wisdom that you have acquired by listening and following God! You are indeed the miracle that has just happened!

Chapter 19

The Conclusion

"In due time, everything will be turned into the nothingness that can only be imagined!"

In conclusion, the end of your journey is not going to be judged based on how you think it will end. God has plans for all of us. Each predestined spirit of God's creation carries with them the same enormity of love and guidance that God has given the Spirit of Man. Man himself is a miracle created by God out of God's pure love and devotion for His Human creation! Human emotion as it is, also displays God's complex emotion, as we are made in the image and likeness of God. With this particular knowledge, we can predict that we are as complex a creation especially when we have to display the complexity of our Creator, who made us in His image and likeness.

The likelihood of judging our future definitely without God in it will be a bleak one! When total darkness will engulf this Planet in the final days, then it will be the end of the spirit of man. And it will be a very dangerous future of mankind!

A future that we should never wish to happen in our lifetime! Our future transcendence will actually depend on how mature we are going to be spiritually. Our journeys will only count if we tread through this life with God in our midst! Without Him, we will be doomed forever to the nothingness that we have become. And it is our very negligence to our responsibilities that made us fall below from our very own higher standards.

It is not too late to begin a new life. We can control our very destiny and future, with the lights and the love from God. Let Him be the guide to pave the way to our paradise. With His love, we will surely be blessed and be saved from the misgivings of this life!

In the future, we will only look forward to our strength that is within us, to help us strengthen our faith journey in this lifetime. God's love for mankind will save the spirit of man from the darkness of his soul. Man will continue to thrive on this planet with the help and guidance from God. If we can only turn around and start a fresh journey to propel our lives to the direction of goodness and righteousness, surely we will be rewarded in the end with the wisdom to also propel ourselves and our spirits to the right directions of our lives!

With the proper use of God's Eternal Tools of Alignment, you will for sure have probably already acquired the gifts that you deserved. And in the due course of time, you will mature your Spirit to fulfill its predestined mission in life! You will definitely be rewarded with the gifts of wisdom that will be rightfully yours if you keep your faith. At this point in your life, you may have been already given the wisdom that was given to you automatically as you followed His will in your life.

As you tread through life, you have become God's favored and gifted child. Your life has changed for the better. As there are still some questions, you now know that you have the wisdom to exercise proper judgment. You will naturally be wiser in the way you control and handle your life.

You will not be caught red handed with all kinds of misgivings anymore, because you have humbly passed your initial test for living life the right way, and have gained God's wisdom to sustain your life in the right direction. With God's wisdom, you are on the way to expect more success in your life and a better outlook for the future. You will also surely become the gem of this planet and a good example for mankind to follow.

You will truly carry the torch of God's life that will get brighter each day that you shine amongst your neighbors, and to the other children of God! The torch that you will carry will always brighten the lives of those who needed such light, to brighten their hearts in the darkness of their lives! You will walk with profound humility that is displayed in your peaceful spirit. Still humble, with so much love and wisdom to share, you have become who you have wished to become for such a long time. You are now also walking with the Holy Spirit because you now have earned God's favors!

As you sojourn from your past lifetime of misery, now your life will be replaced by a renewed vigor and zest for the life of a wonderful adventure with God. Now you will be looking forward to a future with God. The time to change is now and is here at this moment of your time!

As you grow in your spirit and in your heart, your pains and sorrows will not really matter much anymore, because you have realized, that your pain is nothing compared to the One up above, who have created you out of love! With the toils of life and the darkness that is hovering up above, deep down in your heart you knew, that you would survive all kinds of the tests of life, because you have God on your side! And the lights and the love will prevail.

The Eternal Tools of God will be most powerful to help you survive for what is to become, in the future time of your life. The knowledge and the wisdom that you have acquired from this book will have enlightened your mind and your heart to point you to the right directions of your life! Now you are ready as ever to venture into your spiritual and personal journey with the strength that is only special to you!

This time, you are not in fear of the wrong path and destination that will be presented before you in this lifetime, but you will look forward to a natural path that is only for you, and for your spirit. This book will allow you the true knowledge in life, and will pave the way to your very own special spiritual wisdom!

The dark past will be soon forgotten, and will be replaced by the twilight of your present life! With the Eternal Tools from God, you will be ready to face and to choose the right battles of your life. And you will win such battles in your own good time! Come forward and gather more armies for God!

The time is ripe to follow the joyful ways to a new life! A new beginning of positive emotions that will flood the powerful lights and love to heal this ailing World from its darkest flight! Rejoice in the knowledge that God will always be at your side. The time for His glory has arrived and His Eternal Tools of Life has been given to you in a stride! Do not forget Him in your heart, because in the end of your life, you will come to Him full of light!

This is the now and then and the story of your life. Forget your dark past, and replace it with your brightest light of love! Make a difference everywhere your spirit can give light. You are God's greatest glory, when you carry His light in your heart!

In the end, you will have endured this life and you have returned to the loving arms of God! The eventual wisdom that you have gained was the product of your hard work to lift your soul back to God! And like the priceless love that you are to God, you will feel the special bond between you and His Loving and Holy Spirit of truth! Ultimately, you will return to Him that has created you and in His loving arms, you will grow.

In peace and love you will continue to tread your life on this planet, and you will forever grow in His grace and glory of love and mercy for you! In God's loving mercy, you will forever live in peace and in the goodness for mankind to follow. You will exactly represent the ideal example of goodwill between men. An ideal human being almost perfect in oneness with God's spirit in a humble man!

In His mercy, you will free yourself from the evil sins that you have committed. And you will have His favors in your life, because you have welcomed Him in your heart! In the future of this World, when all things will return to nothingness, you will shine before God's eyes and you will become transformed before God's throne! In oneness with God Spirit, you will truly dwell in His Heart! In the darkest moments of your life, you will be carried into the light by the arms of your only Savior in Heaven that is God! Your new positive beginning will pave the way to God's heart. And you will truly become "the Gifted one" by God!

The future of your life will be a brighter one. The darkness of the past will now be replaced with the glorious life of love and of the lights that is imaginable to one who truly deserves his very good life the second time around!

God is the past, the present, and the future of human lives and of this whole planet. With God being absent from any human life, is a total catastrophe and death to the human spirit. Behold! The Kingdom of God is about to come, pray for His mercy, repent and change your ways. God in His Eternal ways has unfold His Eternal Tools of Alignment before you to follow His lead, till the end of your time!

This Earthly existence that we dwell in is just a stage that is set by God, to allow us to play our individual roles. How well we play it, is really up to how well we use our gifts of "freewill". Now that God is calling all of us to change our ways and go back to Him, I am only hoping, that some of us, if not all of us are paying attention to Him!

In the end, as much as we can say that we do not know what is our responsibility towards ourselves, in the future of our lives, we are still expected to know that ignorance will never be accepted as an excuse.

When we have to face God in our final destination of life, He will eventually judge us in the end! There will be questions and there will be doubts. But if you will try to discern, God will provide all the answers for you in the end. Make Him fill you up with the thirst for knowledge and the wisdom that you may have to grow your spirit right!

Finally, I am praying for you to lend God your ears, and listen to Him deeply with your hearts. Discern in what your hungry spirits dictates. Change your ways and surrender your will to God. The future of this World's transformation is inevitable. And you can see the change of the times.

Do not be caught unaware of life's traps to destroy you and your spirit. You will only end up in the confusion and in the desperation that you do not deserve. Simplify your life; if you complicate and cramp your lifestyle with so many unnecessary details in your life, you will only slow the growth of your own spirit. Be very responsible to all your actions towards other people, may it be small or big that you do, make sure to take every bit of responsibility for your actions. In the future, you will pay for your sins in God's own perfect time.

What you do bad, will entitle you and your very own family to carry the burden of repaying it back. Your sins will seek you out no matter where you are going to hide! Remember that in the end, you will be the only one who will dance to your own music and nobody else will do it for you.

You hold your future in your hand. And with God by your side, you will be assured of a good future. But to refuse Him in your life, will be a hard and bleak future to anticipate in your life! Do not get fooled by a fake promise of a wonderland. In this lifetime, you must earn everything! You must work hard to maintain a good and healthy spiritual life! Your life in the end will truly depend on the balance of your mind, body and spirit. A total balance that is only possible, if God is truly in the midst of your daily walks of life!

So fulfill your lifetime mission on this planet, and help God reestablish His Paradise on Earth again! Look forward to a more wonderful reality that is just possible when God comes first in our lives! Together, we will continue to walk in total peace and love in the future. Walking hand in hand with God, we will forever be free of the darkness that surrounds this World. And our lives will be worthwhile living the second time around!

The Eternal Tools of Alignment with God is now revealed before your very eyes to help you, and to guide you, to God's Eternal Kingdom, where you ultimately will return! Earn your merits and be deserving of His gifts, to help and make you stronger in your battles with life! The deeper that you understand your rightful place on this planet, the better it is for your very own soul to grow into a mature spirit to live forever to be with God!

My only wish for you is to search very deep inside your hearts and your inner souls and look for the Spirit of God. Trust that God will soon manifest in your lives, to help all of you, to discern the right path to follow in the direction to His heart!

So let us now fulfill our individual purposes in life, and let us hold on to God's hands, to lead us to a wonderful future with Him in our midst. Let us journey together to the future and meet God and help Him reestablish His Paradise on Earth again!

Let His book, The Eternal Tools open the door to a perfect journey that only God can unlock! Soon God will beckon to you and say, Welcome Home my Perfect Gifted Child!